downtownDIY
Crochet

ALICE CHADWICK
with CLAIRE MONTGOMERIE

downtownDIY Crochet

14 Easy designs for City Girls with Style

Watson-Guptill Publications / New York

Contents

8 tools 10 yarns 12 crochet techniques

20 arm warmers 22 **pretty scarf** 24 mesh

30 FLOWERS *flowers* FLOWERS 34

46 VEST 50 cute winter hood* 53 **THROW**

op - go party girl ! 27 *summer dress*

wrist bag 36 BIKINI 40 BELT 42 skirt

56 SHRUG 60 bluebird lavender cushion

downtownDIY
Crochet

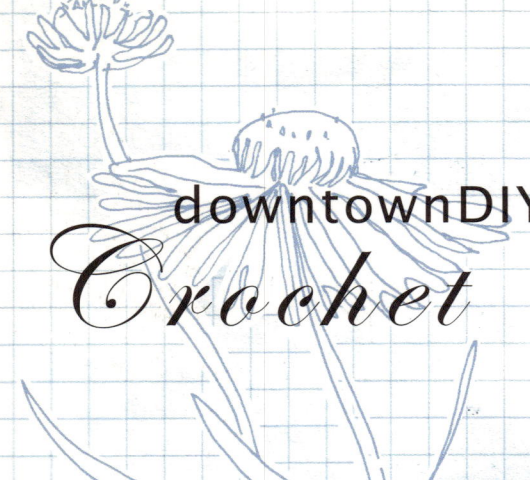

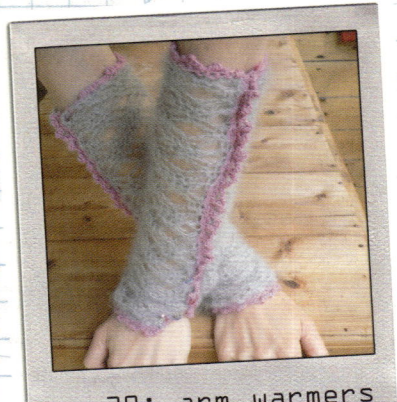
p. 20: arm warmers

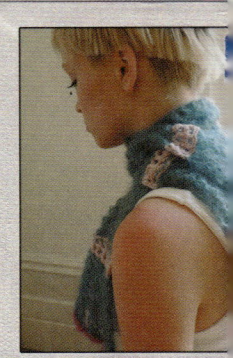
p. 22: scar[f]

p. 30: flowers

p. 34: wrist bag

p. 36: b[ag]

p. 46: vest

p. 50: hood

p. 24: mesh top

p. 27: dress

p. 40: belt

p. 42: skirt

53: throw

p. 56: shrug

p. 60: cushion

Tools

You only need a couple of tools for crochet: yarn (see page 10) and a hook. Hooks come in a range of sizes and materials, including wood, plastic, and metal (aluminum or steel). Bamboo hooks are also popular because they are light and lovely to handle.

A tape measure and a pair of sharp embroidery scissors are also essential.

US	Metric
10 steel	1mm
8 steel	1.25mm
7 steel	1.5mm
B/1	2mm
C/2	2.5mm
C/2	3mm
D/3	3.25mm
E/4	3.5mm
F/5	3.75mm
G/6	4mm
7	4.5mm
H/8	5mm
I/9	5.5mm
J/10	6mm
10¼	6.5mm
K/10½	7mm
L	8mm
N/13	9mm
P/15	10mm

Crochet Hooks Conversion Chart

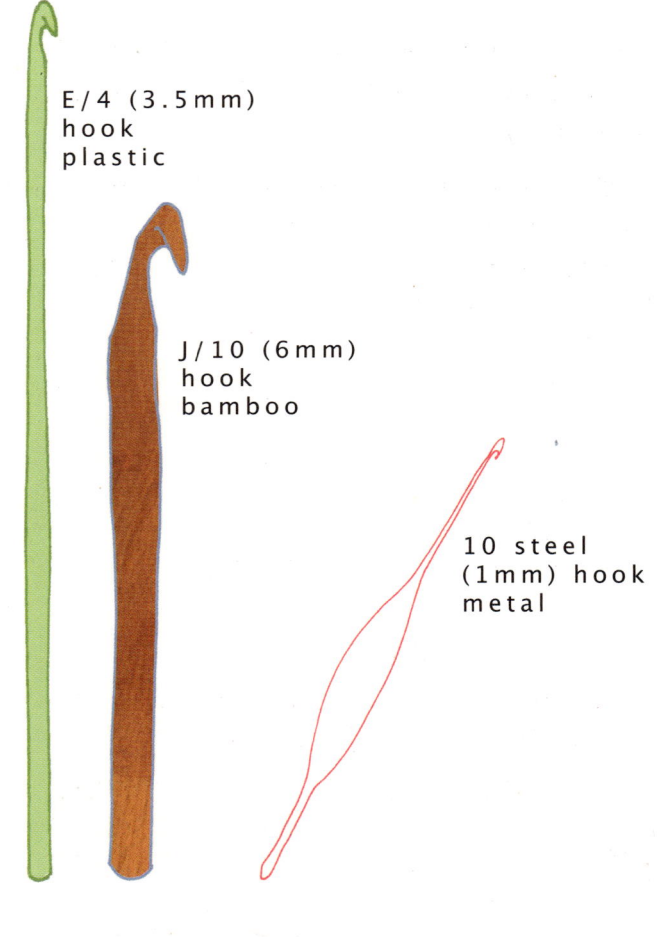

E/4 (3.5mm) hook plastic

J/10 (6mm) hook bamboo

10 steel (1mm) hook metal

& Equipment

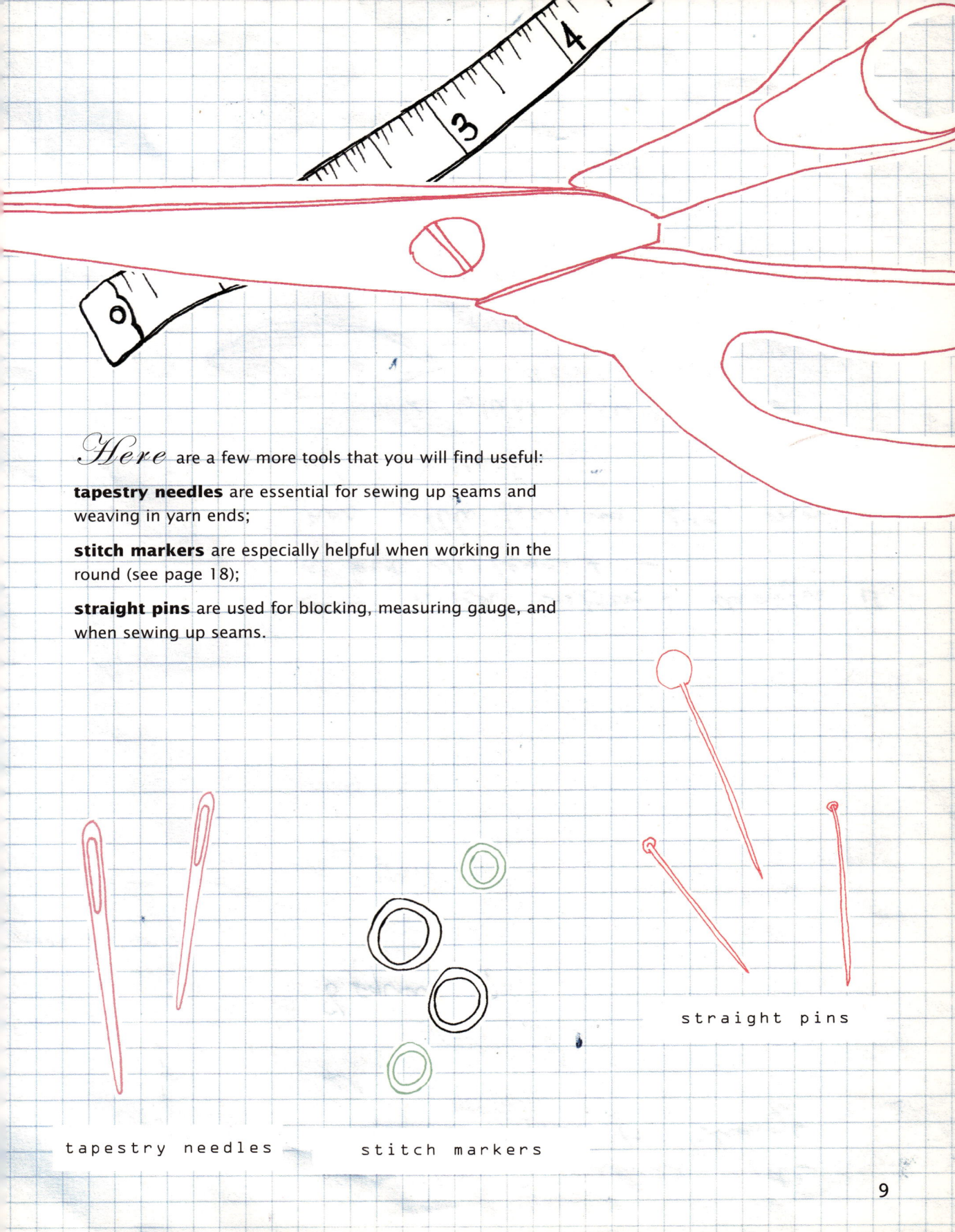

Here are a few more tools that you will find useful:

tapestry needles are essential for sewing up seams and weaving in yarn ends;

stitch markers are especially helpful when working in the round (see page 18);

straight pins are used for blocking, measuring gauge, and when sewing up seams.

tapestry needles   stitch markers   straight pins

Yarns

There are so many types of yarn to choose from—the selection can be both exciting and overwhelming! To make sense of it all, yarn is organized in a few simple ways: the fiber it's made from (such as wool, cotton, or silk), its texture (smooth, bumpy, thick-and-thin), and its thickness, or weight.

    Each pattern in this book calls for a certain type of yarn, then lists the exact brand and color used. If you want to substitute a different color, go for it! And if you want to use a different yarn, that's fine too. The trick is to make sure that the yarn you use is the same basic weight as the one called for in the pattern.

    The Craft Yarn Council of America has designed a system for classifying yarn weights (see the table below). Whenever you want to substitute a yarn, just make sure your yarn is in the same weight category as the one in the pattern. And before you start, *always* knit a swatch to check your gauge, using the same size needles and the same basic stitch pattern used for the body of the project (for more on checking your gauge, see page 17).

The Craft Yarn Council of America's Standard Yarn Weight System

Yarn weight symbol and name of category	1 SUPER FINE	2 FINE	3 LIGHT	4 MEDIUM	5 BULKY	6 SUPER BULKY
Types of yarn	Sock, fingering, baby	Sport, baby	DK, light worsted	Worsted, afghan, aran	Chunky, craft, rug	Bulky, roving
No. of stitches in 4 inches (in single crochet)	21–32 sts	16–20 sts	12–17 sts	11–14 sts	8–11 sts	5–9 sts
Recommended hook sizes (U.S.)	B-1 to E-4	E-4 to 7	7 to I-9	I-9 to K-10 1/2	K-10 1/2 to M-13	M-13 and larger
Recommended hook sizes (metric)	2.25–3.5mm	3.5–4.5mm	4.5–5.5mm	5.5–6.5mm	6.5–9mm	9mm and larger

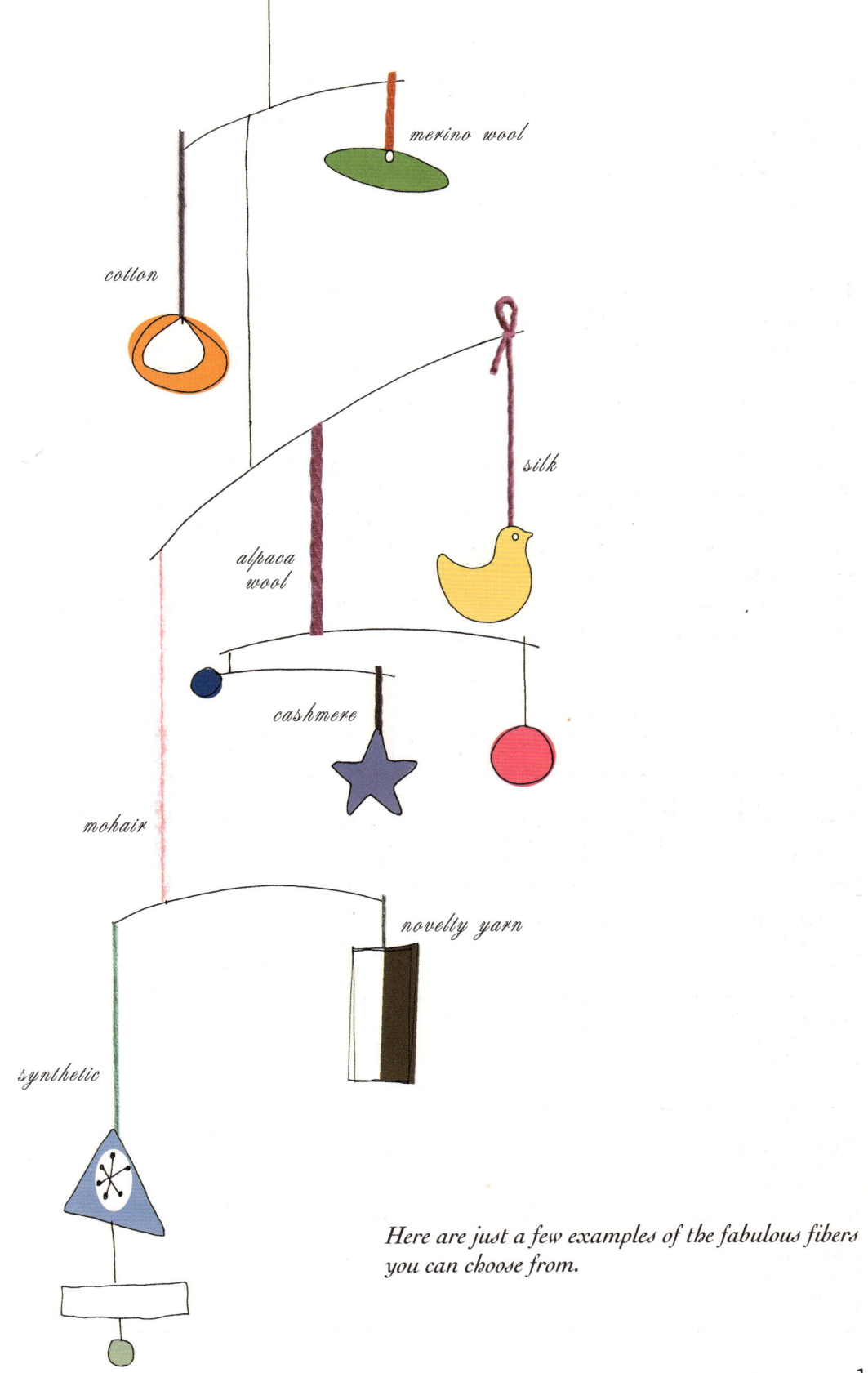

Here are just a few examples of the fabulous fibers you can choose from.

a. holding the hook - method 1

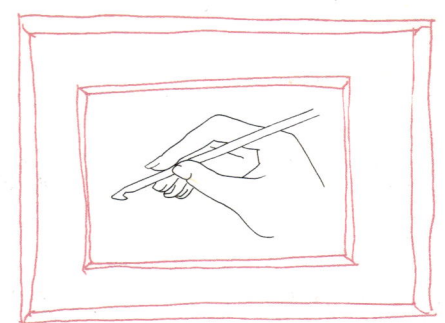
b. holding the hook - method 2

Crochet Techniques

c. holding the yarn - method 1

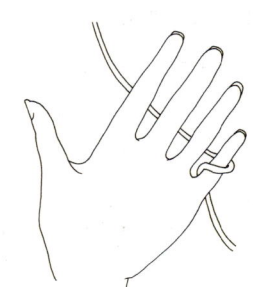
d. holding the yarn - method 2

e. making a slip knot

f.

g.

making a chain

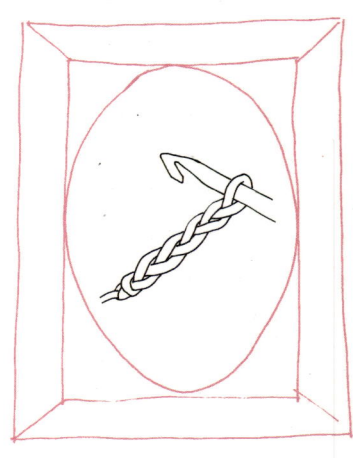
h. completing a chain

How to get started...

It is important to hold the yarn and hook in a correct and comfortable manner to ensure that your gauge (see page 17) is accurate throughout the project. Note, though, that the instructions on these pages are for right-handed working. If you are left-handed, reverse the instructions as appropriate. It may help to view the illustrations in a mirror.

holding the hook & yarn

There are two methods. Choose whichever way feels natural to you.

holding the hook:
1. Hold the hook in your right hand as shown (*illus.* a).
2. Hold the hook in your right hand as you would a pencil (*illus.* b).

holding the yarn:
1. Wrap the working yarn around the little finger of your left hand, passing it under the third and middle fingers and over the index finger, using your index finger to control the tension (*illus.* c).
2. Wrap the working yarn around the little finger of your left hand, passing it over the other three fingers. Hold the work steady with your thumb and index finger and use your middle finger to control the tension (*illus.* d).

making a slip knot
1. Make a loop in the yarn. With hook, grab the working yarn and pull it through the loop (*illus.* e).
2. Pull firmly on yarn and hook to tighten the knot and create first loop.

making a foundation chain
1. Hold tail end of yarn taut. Bring working yarn around hook, from back to front to back again. This is called a yarn over (yo) (*illus.* f).
2. Keeping the tension in yarn taut, draw hook and yarn through the loop on hook (*illus.* g).
3. Pull through, ensuring the stitch is fairly loose. Repeat steps 1 to 3 to make number of chain stitches required in the pattern (*illus.* h).

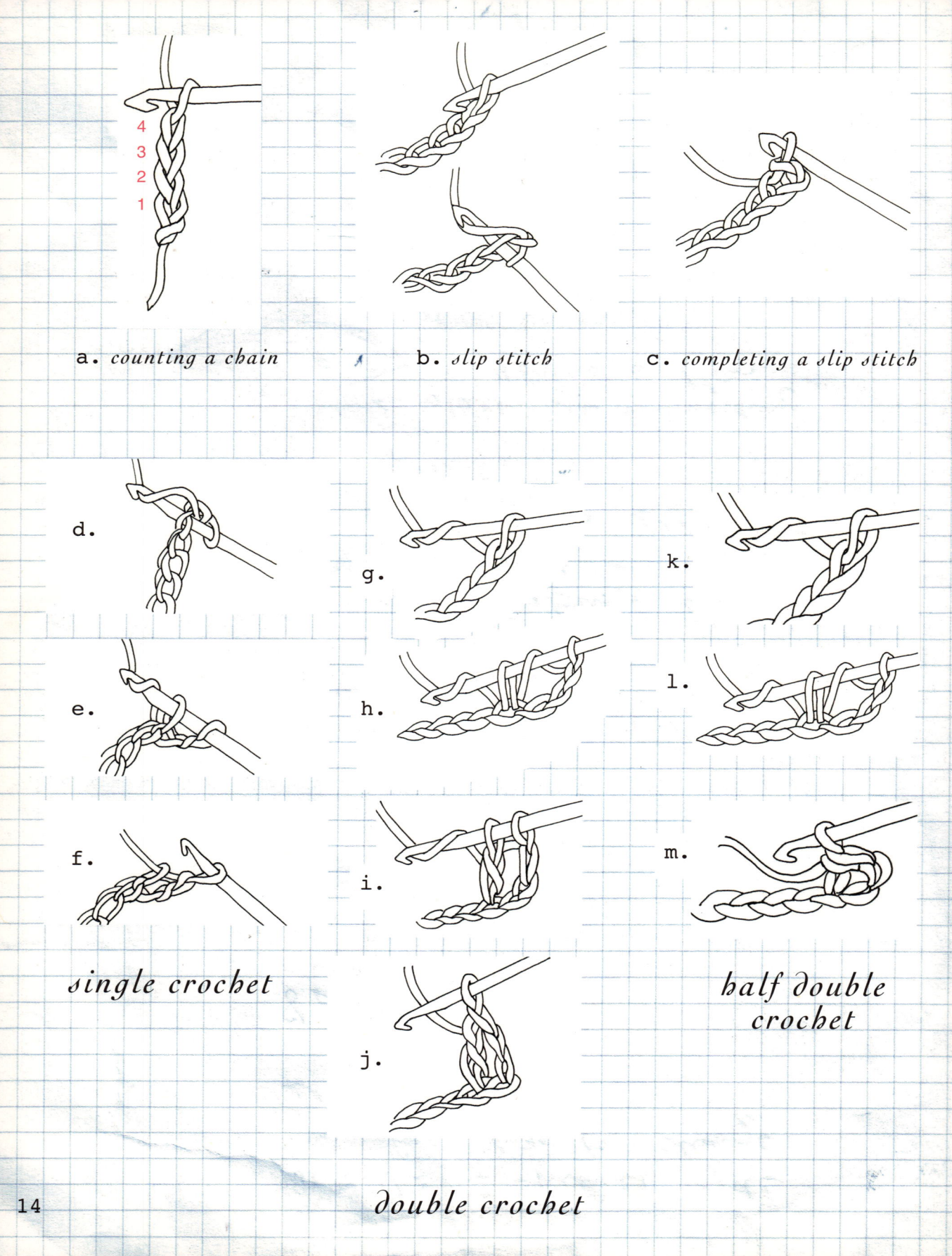

a. *counting a chain*   b. *slip stitch*   c. *completing a slip stitch*

d.   g.   k.

e.   h.   l.

f.   i.   m.

single crochet   j.   *half double crochet*

double crochet

how to count a chain

To count the stitches, use the right side of the chain, or the one that has more visible and less twisted "v" shapes. Don't count the slip stitch; each "v" is one chain (*illus.* a).

making a slip stitch (sl st)

A slip stitch is used for joining motifs or two pieces of crochet together, reinforcing edges, binding off, or taking yarn to another point. Where it is used as a stitch in its own right, you make it by picking up the back loop of the stitch as follows:

1. Insert hook into back loop of next stitch and pass yarn around hook (yo), as you did when making the chain stitch (*illus.* b).
2. Pull yarn through both loops on hook to complete stitch (*illus.* c).

single crochet (sc)

1. Insert hook into next stitch from front to back. Yo (*illus.* d).
2. Pull yarn through to front (two loops are on hook). Yo (*illus.* e).
3. Pull yarn through both loops on hook to complete one sc (*illus.* f).

increasing & decreasing

Increases are made by working two or more stitches into one stitch at either or both ends of the row. Decreases are made by working two or more stitches together as follows:

1. Insert hook into next stitch, yo, and pull loop through.
2. Repeat, inserting hook into next stitch, yo, and pull loop through. (Three loops are on hook.) Yo.
3. Pull hook through all three loops on hook. One single crochet has been decreased.

double crochet (dc)

1. Yo (*illus.* g).
2. Insert hook into fourth chain from hook from front to back, and pull yarn through the stitch only (three loops are on hook). Yo (*illus.* h).
3. Pull yarn through first two loops on hook (two loops are left on hook). Yo (*illus.* i).
4. Pull yarn through remaining two loops on hook to complete one dc (*illus.* j).

half double crochet (hdc)

1. Yo (*illus.* k).
2. Insert hook into fourth chain from hook from front to back, and pull yarn through the stitch only (three loops are on hook). Yo (*illus.* l).
3. Pull yarn through all three loops on hook to complete one hdc (*illus.* m).

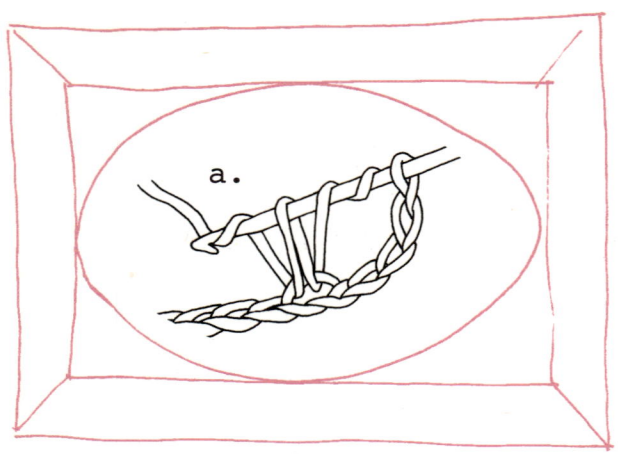

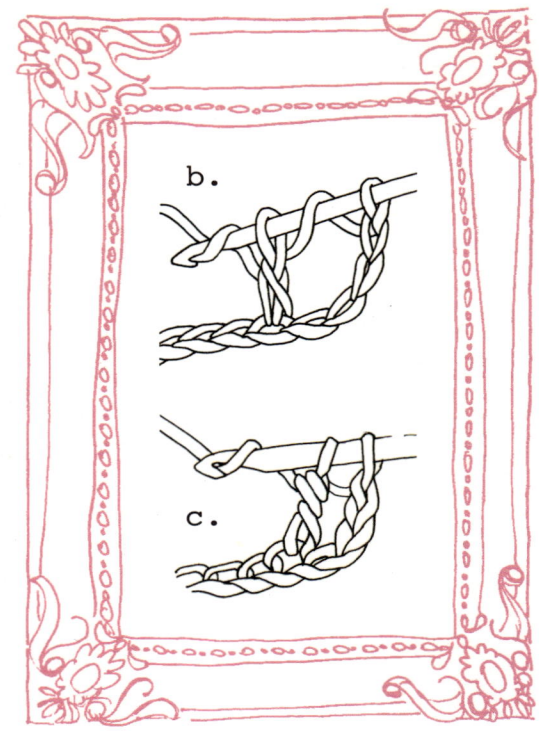

treble crochet

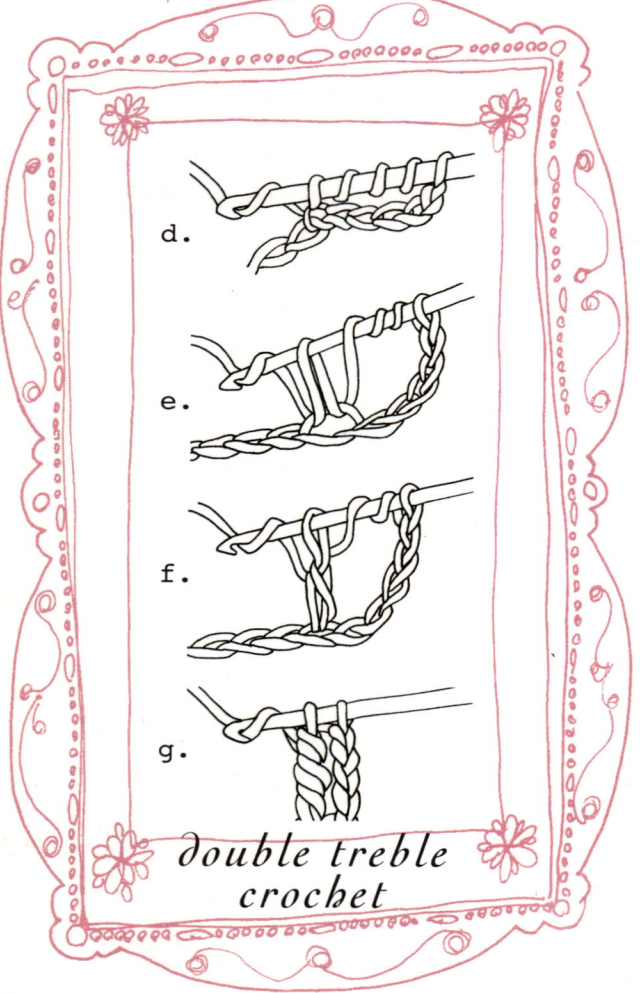

double treble crochet

h. *checking gauge*

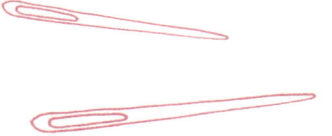

treble crochet (tr)

1. Yo twice. Insert hook into fifth chain from hook. Yo.
2. Pull yarn through stitch to front (four loops are on hook). Yo (*illus.* a).
3. Pull yarn through two loops (three loops are on hook). Yo (*illus.* b).
4. Pull yarn through two loops (two loops are on hook). Yo (*illus.* c). Pull yarn through remaining two loops on hook to complete one tr.

double treble crochet (dtr)

1. Yo three times. Insert hook into sixth chain from hook. Yo (*illus.* d).
2. Pull yarn through stitch to front (five loops are on hook), yo (*illus.* e).
3. Pull yarn through two loops (four loops are on hook), yo (*illus.* f).
4. Pull yarn through two loops (three loops are on hook), yo. Pull yarn through two loops (two loops are on hook). Yo (*illus.* g).
5. Pull yarn through remaining two loops on hook to complete one dtr.

turning a row

At the end of a row, when you turn the work to begin the next row, you must complete a turning chain to get to the height of the stitch you are working. This chain counts as the first stitch in the row, and each basic stitch, depending on its height, uses a different number of chains at the start of the row.

1. After completing a row, turn the work. Yo.
2. Pull yarn through loop on hook and repeat to height of chain required in pattern.

checking your gauge

Before starting, you should make a gauge swatch to ensure that you are crocheting the right number of stitches and rows for a given area of crocheting. This allows you to correct any deviation from the gauge given in the pattern before you begin. The swatch should be approximately 4in./10cm square (*illus.* h).

1. Make a gauge swatch approximately 6 in./15cm square.
2. Measure the swatch 4 in./10cm horizontally along a row. Mark with straight pins.
3. Measure the swatch 4 in./10cm vertically down the rows. Mark with straight pins.
4. Use these sets of markers to count how many stitches and rows there are to 4 in./10cm and compare to the pattern's gauge information. If there are too few stitches or too few rows to the 4 in./10cm square, use a smaller-sized crochet hook. If there are too many stitches or too many rows to 4 in./10cm, use a larger-sized crochet hook.

working in the round

Working in rounds rather than rows means the last stitch of each round is joined by a slip stitch to the first stitch and the work continues in this way, around and around, with no turning (*illus*. a). It's a good idea to use stitch markers to remind you where you started.

making a chain ring

Work a chain as long as required by the pattern (*illus*. b). Join the last chain to the first with a slip stitch (*illus*. c). Begin the first round by working into the center of the circle.

Finishing

Finishing can make or break your project. A good seam should blend perfectly into the work.

fastening off

After finishing the last stitch, cut the yarn, leaving a 6-inch tail (or end) to weave in. Yo. Pull the tail through the loop on the hook, pulling tightly to fasten.

weaving in ends

Thread the yarn onto a tapestry needle and weave this in and out of a few stitches (*illus*. d). Or use a hook to pull the yarn through at least five stitches, winding the yarn over and under to secure it and to make sure that it doesn't work free. Cut off any excess yarn.

slip stitch seam

Place two pieces together, right sides facing. Work a row of slip stitches along the edges of the two pieces, inserting the hook through the back loops only of both pieces (the two loops that touch when the pieces are placed side by side) (*illus*. e).

single crochet seam

Place two pieces together, right sides facing. Work a row of single crochet along the edges of the two pieces, working the single crochet through the stitches of both pieces (*illus*. f).

whipstitch seam

Butt the edges of the two pieces together. With wrong sides faceup and using a tapestry needle, sew through the back loops only of both pieces (the two loops that touch when the pieces are placed side by side) (*illus*. g).

blocking

To block a piece of crochet, lay some padding (such as an old blanket) on a flat surface and cover with a white towel. With wrong side faceup, pin each piece to the required size. Pins should be at right angles to crochet. Spray piece until damp, cover with a clean towel, and pat gently to absorb excess water. Remove towel and let dry.

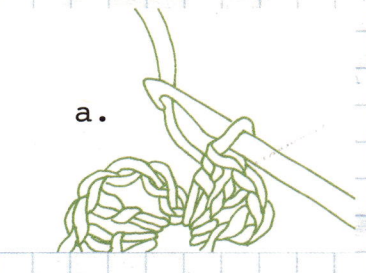

working in the round

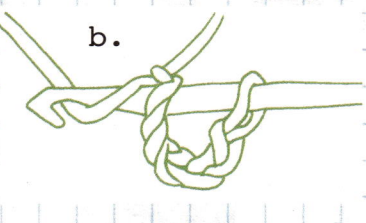 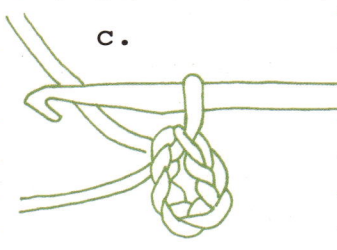

making a chain ring

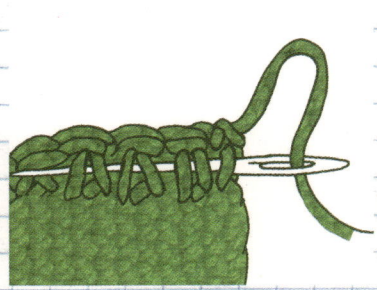 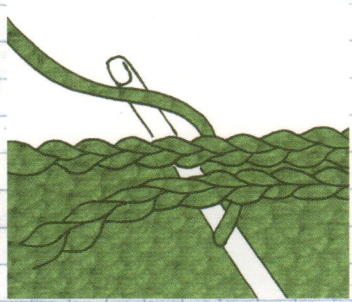

d. *weaving in ends* e. *slip stitch seam*

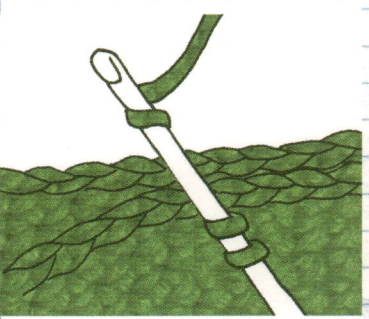 

f. *single crochet seam* g. *whipstitch seam*

Abbreviations

beg	beginning
ch	chain
cont	continue
dc	double crochet
dec	decrease
dtr	double treble crochet
foll	following
hdc	half double crochet
inc	increase
patt	pattern
rep	repeat
sc	single crochet
sk	skip
sl st	slip stitch
sp	space
st(s)	stitch(es)
tr	treble crochet
yo	yarn over
*	repeat instructions after asterisk or between asterisks for as many times as patt indicates
[ ]	repeat instructions between brackets for as many times as patt indicates

These arm warmers are made in a light mohair and use a dreamy lace stitch. Silk edging and little buttons add the glamour, and the stretch in the stitch holds them up. Simple – but aren't they lovely?!

To make the arm warmers

Using yarn A and size 7 (4.5mm) hook, ch 31 (37, 44), turn.
Foundation row: 1sc into 2nd ch from hook and each of foll 2ch, *ch 5, sk 1ch, 1sc into each of next 5ch, rep from *, ending ch 5, 1sc into last 3ch, turn.
Row 1: 1sc into each of first 2sc, *ch 3, 1sc into ch sp of previous row, ch 3, sk 1sc, 1sc into each of next 3sc, rep from *, ending ch 3, 1sc into each of last 2 sts, turn.
Row 2: 1sc into sc, *ch 3, 1sc into ch sp loop, 1sc into sc, 1sc into ch sp loop, ch 3, sk 1sc, 1sc into next sc, rep from *, ending ch 3, 1sc into last sc.
Row 3: 1sc into sc, *1sc into ch sp loop, 3sc into each of next 3sc, 1sc into ch sp loop, ch 5, rep from *, ending 5sc, 1sc into last st.
Row 4: 1sc into sc, *ch 3, 3sc into center 3sc, ch 3, 1sc into ch sp loop, rep from *, ending ch 3, 1sc into last st.
Row 5: 1sc into sc, 1sc into ch sp loop, *ch 3, 1sc into center sc, ch 3, 1sc into ch sp loop, 1sc into sc, 1sc into ch sp loop, rep from *, ending ch 3, 1sc into ch sp loop, 1sc into last st.
Row 6: 1sc into each of next 2sc, 1sc into ch sp loop, *ch 5, 1sc into next ch sp loop, 3sc into next 3sc, 1sc into ch sp loop, rep from *, ending ch 5, 1sc into ch sp loop, 2sc into 2sc.
Work these 6 rows for length of arm warmer, finishing with row 3.
Make 2.

To make the edging

Row 1: Join yarn B to edge, work a multiple of 3sc evenly around edge, turn.
Row 2: *ch 5, sl st to 2nd ch from hook, ch 3, sk 2sc, sc into next st, rep from * around the 2 short sides and one of the long sides. Fasten off.

To finish

Sew long edges together, row of sc to row of sc, being careful not to catch the loose edging, and leaving 3 in./8cm open at bottom. Attach 4 buttons along edge with no second row, use gaps between points in edge for buttonholes.

what you need:

tools:
size 7 (4.5mm) crochet hook
tapestry needle
sewing needle & thread

materials:
Yarn A: 2 x 1¾ oz./50g balls light-weight mohair
*we used Rowan Kid Silk Night, shade 608 in Moonlight (70% super kid mohair, 30% silk)
Yarn B: 1 x 1¾ oz./50g ball DK yarn
*we used Debbie Bliss Pure Silk, shade 10 in Pink (100% silk)
8 buttons

gauge:
12 sts = 4 in./10cm (approximate)

measurements:
length = 12 in./30cm (not including edging)

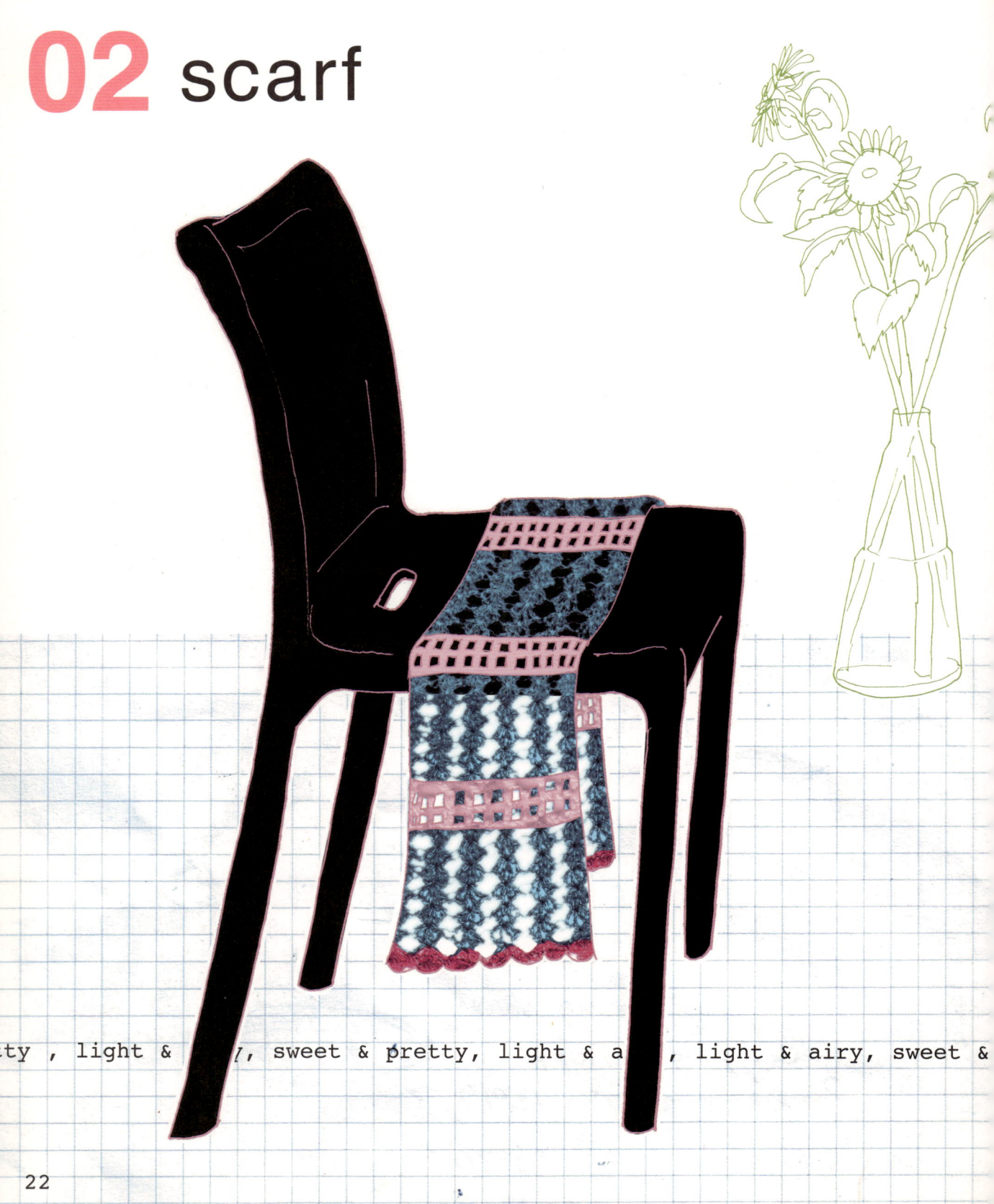

02 scarf

Practice your technique with these repeating sections, then put them together, and hey! You have a *very* beautiful scarf. The shell stitch used here creates a floaty, delicate fabric (the mohair is so soft!) – a perfect complement to the simple lines of the worsted yarn sections.

To make the scarf

Using yarn A and size G/6 (4mm) hook, ch 31, turn.

Row 1: Into 7th ch from hook, work [1dc, ch 1] 3 times and then 1dc (shell made), *sk ch 3, into next chain work another shell as before, rep from * to last 4ch, sk ch 3, 1dc into next ch, ch 3, turn. 6 shells.

Row 2: 1 shell into center ch sp of first shell, *1 shell into center ch sp of next shell, rep from * to last shell, shell into center ch sp of next shell, sk next ch sp of same shell, 1dc into next ch, ch 3, turn. 6 shells.

Rep row 2 six more times (8 rows). Fasten off yarn A, turn.

Attach yarn B and use size C/2 (2.5mm) hook for next 3 rows.

Row 9: Sl st 48 sts evenly across shells of previous row, turn.

Row 10: Ch 6, sk next 3 sl sts, work 1dc into next sl st, *ch 3, sk 3 sl sts, 1dc into next sl st, rep from * across row, turn. 12 filet squares.

Row 11: Ch 6, work 1dc into next dc, *ch 3, 1dc into next dc, rep from * across row, working last dc into 3rd st of 6ch at beg of previous row. Fasten off yarn B.

Using size G/6 (4mm) hook, attach yarn A to opposite end of row.

Row 12: Ch 3, work 1 shell into top of next dc, *sk 1dc, work one shell into top of next dc, rep from * to last dc, 1dc into last dc, ch 3, turn. 6 shells.

Row 13: 1 shell into center ch sp of first shell, *1 shell into center ch sp of next shell, rep from * to last shell, shell into center ch sp of next shell, sk next ch sp of same shell, 1dc into next ch, ch 3, turn. 6 shells.

what you need:

tools:
sizes G/6 & C/2 (4mm & 2.5mm) crochet hooks
tapestry needle

materials:
Yarn A: 1 x 1 oz./25g ball fine mohair
*we used Rowan Kid Silk Haze, shade 582, Trance (70% super kid mohair, 30% silk)
Yarn B: 1 x 1¾ oz./50g ball worsted yarn
*we used Debbie Bliss Alpaca Silk, shade 20 in Pink (80% alpaca, 20% silk)
Yarn C: 1 x 1¾ oz./50g ball fine mohair
*we used Rowan Kid Silk Haze, shade 606, Candy Girl (70% super kid mohair, 30% silk)

gauge:
Not critical for this project

measurements:
39 in./98cm long x 6¾ in./17cm wide
blue section = 4¾ in./12cm (l) x 6¾ in./17cm (w)
pink section = 1¼ in./3cm (l) x 6¾ in./17cm (w)

Rows 14–19: Rep row 13.

Rows 9–19 form patt. Rep these rows 12 more times, omitting last ch 3 on last row. Fasten off.

To make the edging

Use yarn C and size G/6 (4mm) hook.

Join yarn to last row, 1sc into first sp, *1 shell into shell, 1sc into next sp, rep from * to end, 1sc into last st. Fasten off.

Join yarn C to foundation row, 1sc into first st, 1 shell into bottom of first shell, *1sc into sp, 1 shell into bottom of next shell, rep from * to end, 1sc into last st. Fasten off.

To finish

Weave in loose ends (see page 18).

This top is irresistible! Solomon's knots are fun to make and create a gorgeous, loopy lace. Try a yarn with a sheen and add a few sequins or beads. Let yourself shine!

To make the back

Using size E/4 (3.5mm) hook, ch 88 (96, 104).
Row 1: Work 2 Solomon's knots, *sk 7ch, sl st into next ch, work 2 knots, rep from * to end. Work 3 knots, turn.
Row 2: Sk turning 3 knots, 1sc into center of next unjoined knot of previous row, *2 knots, 1sc into center of next unjoined knot of previous row, rep from * to end, Work 3 knots, turn. Rep row 2 until work measures 18 in./46cm.
Next row: Sk turning 3 knots, 1sc into center of next unjoined knot of previous row, *1 knot, 1sc into center of unjoined knot of previous row, rep from * once more. Fasten off.
Join yarn to last row of opposite outside edge, work 3 knots and work into 3 unjoined knots as for previous row on other side.

what you need:

tools:
size E/4 (3.5mm) crochet hook
tapestry needle
sewing needle & thread

materials:
3 x 1¾ oz./50g balls DK yarn
*we used ggh Mystik (54% cotton, 46% rayon), shade 97 in Petrol Blue
sequins or beads (optional)

gauge:
1 Solomon's knot motif = 2 in./5cm

measurements:
sizes = small (medium, large)
bust = 32 in./81cm (34 in./86cm, 36 in./91cm)

Note: Be careful when measuring the fabric, as the garment may hang longer when draped.

TO MAKE A SOLOMON'S KNOT

Start with a ch with multiple of 8.
01: *Pull up loop on hook to height of approximately ¾ in. (2cm) and pull a loop through loop on hook, holding extended loop firmly with left hand to maintain height of loop.
02: Insert hook from front to back into back loop only, yo and pull loop through (2 loops on hook). Yo and pull both loops on hook through.
03: 1 Solomon's knot made.
Note: Practice maintaining the gauge so that all loops are of equal size.

To make the front

Work as for back until work measures 16 in./41cm.
Next row: Sk turning 3 knots, 1sc into center of next unjoined knot of previous row, *1 knot, 1sc into center of unjoined knot of previous row, rep from * once more, turn. 3 knots.
Work 2 more rows only on the knots worked in this row. Fasten off.
Join yarn to last row of opposite outside edge, work 3 knots and work into 3 unjoined knots for 3 rows as for other side. Fasten off.

To make the sleeves

Using size E/4 (3.5mm) hook, ch 80.
Work in patt as for back and front until work measures 14 in./36cm. Fasten off.
Make 2.

To finish

Join shoulder seams by sewing center sc of corresponding unjoined knots together. Sew sleeves to armholes in same way, then sew up side and sleeve seems in same way. Using tapestry needle, weave in loose ends.

To make the edging

Join yarn to any knot on neck edge.
Round 1: *Ch 5, 1sc into next knot, rep from * around neck edge, joining at end of round with a sl st.
Round 1: Work sc into each st of first round. Work rounds 1 and 2 around edges of body and sleeves.

Glitz it up:
Sew sequins or beads onto the knots

what you need:

tools:
size C/2 (2.5mm) crochet hook
tapestry needle

materials:
10 x 1¾ oz./50g balls DK yarn
*we used Rowan Cotton Glace, shade 816 in Mocha Choc (100% mercerized cotton)
1 button

gauge:
1 circle = 4 in./10cm

measurements:
bust = 35 in./90cm
dress length = 35 in./90cm

What can beat a simple shift for elegance? Made with 64 circles connected by lengths of chain, this dress has the cutest peephole back, fastened with a single button. Perfect over a slip, bikini, or jeans—or for a bike ride!

To make the circle motif

Using size C/2 (2.5mm) hook, ch 4, sl st into first ch to make ring.

Round 1: Ch 1, 10sc into ring.

Round 2: Ch 5, *1dc into back loop of next sc, ch 3, rep from * all around, join with sl st to 3rd st of foundation ch. 10dc.

Round 3: Ch 3, 1dc into next ch sp, *ch 2, 1dc into next dc, 2dc into next ch sp, rep from * all around, ending ch 2, 1dc into next dc, join round with sl st to top of first 3ch. 30dc, 10 ch sp.

Round 4: Ch 7, *sk ch sp, 1dc into center dc of next group of 3, ch 4, rep from * all around, join round with sl st into 3rd st of foundation ch.

Round 5: Ch 3, *2dc into next ch sp, ch 2, 2dc into same ch sp, 1dc into dc, rep from * all around, ending with 2dc into ch sp, join round with sl st into top of first 3ch. 50dc, 10ch sp. Fasten off.

As each circle is made, join it to previous one with sl st to center top dc, fasten off, and weave in loose ends. Cont in this way until there are four 7-circle-long strips for back and four 9-circle-long strips for front (64 circles needed in total).

Take two 7-circle-long strips to begin the joining for back, starting at bottom of strips and working upward, as follows:

Foundation row: Ch 24, turn, attach ch with sl st to bottom left ch sp of bottom circle in one strip, ch 4, sk 4ch of foundation ch, sc into next ch, ch 8, sk 4ch, 1sc into next ch, ch 8, sk 4ch, 1sc into next ch, ch 4, sl st into bottom right ch sp of bottom circle in other 7-circle-long strip, ch 4, 1sc into first ch of foundation ch turn, sl st back along 4ch to ch sp of circle.

Row 1: *Ch 4, 1sc into next ch sp clockwise around circle, ch 4, 1 sc into next 8ch sp, ch 8, 1sc into next 8ch sp, ch 4, sl st into next ch sp counterclockwise around circle, turn.

Row 2: Ch 8, 1sc into next 8ch sp, ch 8, sl st into same ch sp already worked, turn.

Rep these 2 rows until you have worked into the 2 facing top ch sps of both bottom circles.

Next row: Ch 88, 1sc into 8ch sp, ch 8, sl st into ch sp already worked, ch 4, turn.

Next row: Sl st into ch sp directly above in next circle up, ch 4, 1sc into next 8ch sp, ch 8, 1sc into next ch sp, ch 4, sl st into bottom ch sp directly above last circle, ch 8, turn.

Next row: 1sc into next 8ch sp, ch 8, sl st into ch sp already worked.

Next rows: As rows 1 and 2, rep this latticework to join all 14 circles in these 2 strips, moving from circle to circle vertically as above. Fasten off when facing ch sps of top 2 circles have been worked. Pick up another 7-circle-long strip and join in the same way to the right of 2 strips just joined, attaching yarn to 20th st of starting ch of previous strips and working the foundation row.
When these 4 strips have been joined, pick up the first 9-circle-long strip for front and attach to right of back 4 strips in the same way. Fasten off when top ch sp of 7-circle-long strip has been worked, leaving 2 top circles of 9-circle-long strip unjoined. Join 3 more 9-circle-long strips in the same way, working to the top of the 9 circles. When these 64 circles have been joined into a fabric, block fabric (see page 18). Create tube for dress by joining first 7-circle-long strip to last 9-circle-long strip in the same way as each strip has been joined previously.

To make the back yoke

Attach yarn to center ch sp of joining latticework between center 2 circles at top of back.
Row 1: With right side faceup, ch 8, 1sc into next ch sp, ch 8, 1sc into center dc at top of next circle, ch 8, 1sc into next ch sp, ch 8, 1sc into next ch sp, ch 8, 1sc into next ch sp, ch 8, 1sc into center dc at top of next circle, turn.
Row 2: Sl st into center of last ch sp of previous round. *Ch 8, 1 sc into next ch sp, rep from * to end of row.
Rep last row 5 more times.
Dec row: Sl st into center of last ch sp of previous round, *ch 8, 1sc into next ch sp, rep from * to last 2 ch sps, ch 8, 1sc into next ch sp, turn, leaving last ch sp unworked.
Next row: Rep row 2.
Dec row: Sl st into center of last ch sp of previous round, *ch 8, 1sc into next ch sp, rep from * to last 2 ch sps, ch 8, 1sc into next ch sp, turn, leaving last ch sp unworked. Fasten off.
Rep instructions for opposite side of yoke, starting with wrong side faceup.

Attach shoulders by sewing back yoke shoulder seam to front, starting from center dc at top of top circle on edge of front, then straight across toward neck edge for 2½ in./6cm.

To finish

Neck edge trim: Join yarn to neck edge and work 1 row of sc evenly all around edge. At left corner of yoke, work (1sc, ch 8, 1sc) into next st to make loop to act as buttonhole, then cont around edge as before. Join last st with sl st into first st of round. Fasten off.
Attach button to right corner of yoke to correspond with buttonhole loop.

Hem trim: Join yarn to any point around edge of hem and work 1 row of sc evenly around edge, join row with sl st into first st of round.

Armhole edges: Join yarn to any point around edge of armhole and work 1 row of sc evenly around edge, using the row to join together outer edges of top 2 circles on either side of front in the foll way: work sc around edge of circle, upon reaching the last unworked ch sp before next circle, ch 4 and then join this ch with sl st to first unworked ch sp of circle below and cont working sc around edge of lower circle and rest of armhole. Join row with sl st to first st of rnd.
Give dress a final light press.

05 flowers

flowers
flowers

flower 2

flower 3

flower 1

30

Flowers, flowers, flowers . . . everybody needs a little bit of summer in their wardrobe. Put them in your hair, on your bag, on your best friend's favorite jacket. So simple to make and perfect for using up all the scraps of yarn you can find. Try using different weights and colors, shiny yarns, fluffy yarns—oh, anything you like.

To make flower 1

Approx 2½ in./6cm in diameter

Using yarn A and size C/2 (2.5mm) hook, ch 8 and join with a sl st into first ch.

Round 1: Ch 3, 1dc into ring, *ch 8, 3dc into ring, rep from * 3 more times, ch 8, 1dc into ring, join with sl st to top of first 3ch. 5 petals.

Round 2: Ch 1, *[3sc, 1hdc, 10dc, 1hdc, 3sc] into next petal arch, sl st into each of next 3dc, rep from * all around 4 other petals. Fasten off.

To make flower 2

Approx 4 in./10cm in diameter

Using yarn B and size 7 (4.5mm) hook, ch 5 and join with a sl st to first ch.

Round 1: Ch 3, 1dc into ring, *ch 10, 3dc into ring, rep from * 3 more times, ch 10, 1dc into ring, join with sl st to top of first 3ch. 5 petals.

Round 2: Ch 1, *20sc into next petal arch, sl st into each of next 3dc, rep from * all around 4 other petals. Fasten off.

To make flower 3

Approx 4 in./11cm in diameter

Using yarn C and size G/6 (4mm) hook, ch 8 and join with a sl st to first ch.

Round 1: Ch 3, 1dc into ring, *ch 10, 3dc into ring, rep from * 3 more times, ch 10, 1dc into ring, join with sl st to top of first 3ch. 5 petals.

Round 2: Ch 1, *[3sc, 1hdc, 10dc, 1hdc, 3sc] into next petal arch, sl st into each of next 3dc, rep from * all around 4 other petals. Fasten off.

---

what you need:

tools:
sizes 7, G/6, & C/2 (4.5mm, 4mm, & 2.5mm) crochet hooks
tapestry needle
size 35 (19mm) knitting needle

materials:

Yarn A: 1 x 1¾ oz./50g ball DK yarn
*we used ggh Scarlett, shade 31 in Fuchsia (100% Egyptian cotton)

Yarn B: 1 x 1¾ oz./50g ball worsted yarn
*we used Debbie Bliss Alpaca Silk, shade 301 in Black (80% alpaca, 20% silk)

Yarn C: 1 x 1¾ oz./50g ball DK yarn
*we used Debbie Bliss Cotton Cashmere, shade 26 in Green (85% cotton, 15% cashmere)

Yarn D: 1 x 1¾ oz./50g ball worsted yarn
*we used Debbie Bliss Alpaca Silk, shade 14 in Brown (80% alpaca, 20% silk)

Yarn E: 1 x 1¾ oz./50g ball worsted yarn
*we used Debbie Bliss Alpaca Silk, shade 18 in Teal (80% alpaca, 20% silk)

Yarn F: 1 x 1¾ oz./50g ball worsted yarn
*we used Debbie Bliss Alpaca Silk, shade 20 in Pink (80% alpaca, 20% silk)

brooch backs
buttons, beads, pins (optional)

gauge:
Not critical for this project

To make flower 4

Approx 3½ in./9cm in diameter

Using yarn D and size 7 (4.5mm) hook, wrap yarn around 2 fingers (or knitting needle) 18 times.
Round 1: Work 24sc into ring made evenly so all wrapped yarn is covered, join with sl st to first sc. Fasten off.
Round 2: Join in yarn E,*ch 8, sk 3sc, 1 sl st into next sc, rep from * 5 more times, ending with sl st into bottom of first ch. 6 loops.

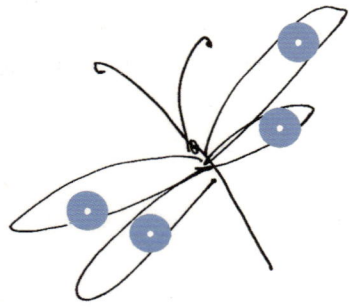

Round 3: *[1sc, 1hdc, 10dc, 1hdc, 1sc] into first loop sp, sl st to sl st, rep from * for next 5 ch loops. 6 petals. Fasten off.
Round 4: Join in yarn F and work 1sc into each st around edge of petals. Fasten off.

To make flower 5

Approx 6 in./15cm in diameter

Using yarn C and size G/6 (4mm) hook, ch 4 and join with sl st to first ch.
Round 1: 8sc into ring, join with sl st to first sc.
Round 2: Ch 1, 2sc into each of next sc. 16 sts.
Round 3: Ch 1, 2sc into each of next sc. 32 sts. Fasten off.
Round 4: Join in yarn F, ch 1, and work sc all around. 32 sts.

flower 4

Round 5: Join in yarn E. Work 3hdc into the front loop only of each sc all around. Fasten off.

Round 6: Join in yarn F. Working into back loop of round 4 all around, 1sc into each of next 2 sts, *2sc into next sc, 1sc into each of next 2 sts, rep from * to end of round.
Join with sl st to first sc. 42 sts. Fasten off.

Round 7: Ch 1, work one round even of sc. 42 sts.
Round 8: Ch 1, 1sc into each of next 3 sts, *2sc into next sc, 1sc into each of next 3 sts, rep from * to end of round, ending with 1sc into last 2 sc. Join with sl st to first sc. 52 sts.
Round 9: Ch 4, sk next sc, *1hdc into next sc, ch 2, rep from * to end of round, ending with sl st to 2nd of first ch. 26 hdc.
Round 10: *1sc, 1hdc, 2dc, 5tr, 2dc, 1hdc, 1sc into next consecutive 13sc, rep from * 5 more times, sl st into first sc to close round. 6 petals. Fasten off.

flower 5

To finish

Weave in loose ends (see page 18). Attach brooch back to reverse side of each flower.
You can decorate the centers of the flowers with buttons, beads, and pins.

06 bag

We used silk here to make this wrist bag—fabulous for day, even better for night. The bobbles on the flap look impressive, but are easy-peasy (sssshhh!) and fun to make.

what you need:

tools:
size E/4 (3.5mm) crochet hook
tapestry needle
sewing needle & thread

materials:
Yarn A: 3 x 1¾ oz./50g balls DK yarn
*we used Debbie Bliss Pure Silk, shade 10 in Pink (100% silk)
Yarn B: 1 x 1 oz./25g ball metallic yarn
*we used Twilleys Goldfingering in Silver (80% viscose, 20% metallized polyester)
brooch to fasten

gauge:
18 sts & 11 rows = 4 in./10cm

To make the bag

Using yarn A and size E/4 (3.5mm) hook, ch 52, turn.
Row 1: 1dc into 4th ch from hook, dc to end, ch 3, turn. 49 dc.
Row 2: Dc to end, ch 3, turn. 49 sts.
Rep row 2 until work measures 10¾ in./27cm.
Make bobble (B1) on foll rows:
Row 1: 3dc, *B1 into next st, 1dc into next st, rep from * to last 2 sts, 1dc into each st, ch 3, turn.
Row 2: Dc to end, ch 3, turn.
Rep these 2 rows once more.
Row 5: As row 1.
Row 6: As row 2, but dec one st at either end, ch 3, turn. 47 sts.
Row 7: Dec one st at beg of row, 1dc into next st, *B1 into next st, 1dc into next st, rep from * to last 4 sts, 1dc into each of next 2 sts, dec 1 st. 45 sts. Fasten off.

To finish

Fold over the dc end of the work (not the end with bobbles) so that folded edge measures about 4¼ in./11cm. Sew up either side of this edge for side seam. Join yarn A to edge and work one row of sc evenly all around unsewn edges of flap and bag, join with a slip st to first st. Fasten off.

To make the handle

Using yarn A and size E/4 (3.5mm) hook, ch 200. Fasten off. Use this length of ch to make another chain. Attach this ch in a loop to one end of bag. Attach brooch to flap to fasten bag.
Alternatively, make a longer handle and attach to top of bag at either end of flap.

TO MAKE A BOBBLE (B1)

Work a number of half-completed sts into 1 st. Here we use multiples of half-completed dc sts, made into 1 st as follows: [yo, insert hook into next st, yo, pull yarn through, yo, pull through 2 loops but do not pull though last 2 loops] 8 times. 9 loops on hook. Yo, pull yarn through 8 loops, yo, pull loop through last 2 loops on hook. Bobble made (**B1**).

This is a bikini in a classic, flattering style, with a cute little frill just for fun. Use a yarn with a bit of stretch in it (a nylon or Tactel blend) and make yourself a beach legend.

To make the bottom

Work the bikini bottom in yarn A throughout, joining in yarn B for row 7 and 7th row from end only to create one stripe that continues around the bikini bottom.
Using size E/4 (3.5mm) hook, ch 49 (53, 57).
Row 1: 1sc into 2nd ch from hook, *1sc into next ch, rep from * to end, ch 1, 48 (52, 56) sc, turn.
Row 2: 1sc into each of next sc to end, ch 1, 48 (52, 56) sc, turn.
Rep row 2 once (twice, 3 times) more, dec 2 sts at either end of the row(s), turn. 44 sts.
Cont in sc, dec 1 st at either end of each row until 13 sts remain.
Work 16 more rows evenly in sc on these 13 sts.
Cont in sc, inc 1 st at either end of each row until there are 95 (99, 103) sts. Fasten off.
Attach yarn to one corner of bikini bottom, ch 100, turn and work 1sc into each ch, sl st into first ch to join. Fasten off. Rep at rem three corners to make ties.

what you need:

tools:
size E/4 (3.5mm) crochet hook
tapestry needle

materials:
It is important to use a yarn with some nylon, Tactel, or stretch in it
*we used Gedifra Colorito (52% Tactel, 25% viscose, 23% cotton)
Yarn A: 5 (5, 6) x 1¾ oz./50g balls worsted yarn
*we used Gedifra Colorito, shade 6914 in Black
Yarn B: 1 x 1¾ oz./50g ball worsted yarn
*we used Gedifra Colorito, shade 6903 in White
Yarn C: 1 x 1¾ oz./50g ball worsted yarn
*we used Gedifra Colorito, shade 6944 in Pink

gauge:
17sc = 4 in./10cm

measurements:
sizes = small (medium, large)
bust = 32 in./81cm (34 in./86cm, 36 in./91cm)
hips = 35 in./89cm, (36 in./91cm, 38 in./96cm)

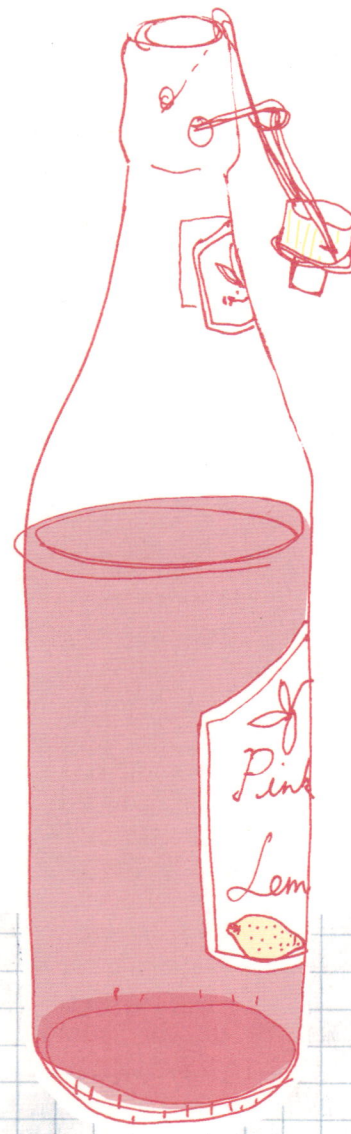

To make the top

Using yarn A and size E/4 (3.5mm) hook, ch 15, turn.

Row 1: 1sc into 2nd ch from hook, working through one loop only, 1sc into each ch to end, working through one loop only. Turn and work along other side of ch, 2sc into next ch, 1sc into each ch to end, through unworked other loop of ch, ch 2, turn. 29 sc.

Row 2: Work [1hdc into each of next 12 sc, 2dc into next sc, 5dc] (1 cluster made) into next sc, 2dc into next sc, 1hdc into each sc to end, ch 2, turn. 35 sts.

Row 3: Ch 2, 1hdc into each st to end, turn.

Row 4: Ch 2, 1hdc into each of next 15 sts, 2dc into next st, 1 cluster into next st, 1hdc into each st to end, ch 2, turn. 41 sts.

Row 5: As row 3.

Row 6: 1hdc into each of next 18 sts, 2dc into next st, 1 cluster into next st, 1hdc into each st to end, ch 2, turn. 47 sts.

Row 7: As row 3.

Row 8: 1hdc into each of next 21 sts, 2dc into next st, 1 cluster into next st, 1hdc into each st to end, ch 2, turn. 53 sts.

Row 9: 1hdc into each of next 21 sts, 1dc into each of next 9 sts, 1hdc into each st to end, ch 2, turn. 53 sts.

Row 10: 1hdc into each of next 24 sts, 2dc into next st, 1 cluster into next st, 1hdc into next st to end, ch 2. 59 sts.

Cont in this way, inc 6 sts on every alternate row until lower (straight) edge of cup measures about 5½ (6, 6¼) in./14 (15, 16) cm, ending with a cluster row. Fasten off.
Make 2.
Ch 100, with right side faceup, join ch to lower edge of one cup and work 24 (28, 32) sc along straight edge, which will pull edge in slightly. Work 4ch then attach yarn to other cup with right side faceup and work 24 (28, 32) sc along straight edge, ch 100, turn and work 1sc along all lengths of ch and sts along lower edges of cups. Fasten off.
Attach yarn to top point of one cup, ch 100, turn and work 1sc along length of ch, finishing with sl st into first st. Fasten off. Rep with other cup. Weave in loose ends and block (see page 18).

To make the edging

Using size E/4 (3.5mm) hook, attach yarn C to top edge of front of bikini bottom, work 1 row sc evenly along edge, turn, work [1dc, ch 2, 1dc, ch 2, 1dc (1 scallop made) into next sc, *sk 1sc, work 1sc into next st, sk 1sc, work 1 scallop into each st to end, finishing with sc into last st. Fasten off. Rep along top edge of back of bikini bottom and along inside neck edges of bikini top.

Press edging lightly into place, folding it down onto the right side of work.

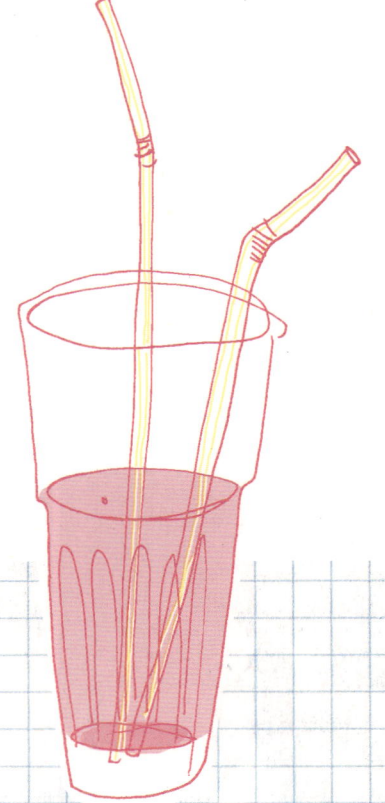

08 belt

Need a belt?
YOU GOT A BELT!

Make it skinny ~
Make it wide.

Make 2!

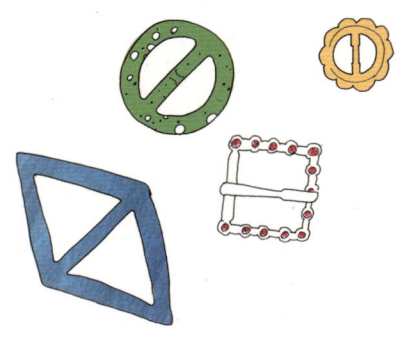

These belts are uber-HIP, sparkly, and very simple to make – perfect for beginners or when you want something a little glam and you need it NOW! The two glitter yarns are used together throughout, making the work fast and creating strong, simple shapes.

what you need:

tools:
size 7 (4.5mm) crochet hook
tapestry needle
sewing needle

materials:
Yarn A: 1 x 1¾ oz./50g ball metallic yarn
*we used Twilleys Goldfingering, shade 51 in Green (80% viscose, 20% metallized polyester)
Yarn B: 1 x 1¾ oz./50g ball metallic yarn
*we used Twilleys Goldfingering, shade 34 in Green (80% viscose, 20% metallized polyester)
belt buckle to fit width of belt

gauge:
1 V st (1dc, ch 3, 1dc) = ½ in./1cm

measurements:
wide = 4 in./10cm (w) x 35 in./90cm (l)*
skinny = ¾ in./2cm (w) x 35 in./90cm (l)*
*or adjust length to fit

To make the wide belt

Using yarns A and B together throughout and size 7 (4.5mm) hook, ch 20, turn.
Row 1: [1dc, ch 3, 1dc] into 5th ch from hook, *sk 2ch, into next chain work [1dc, ch 3, 1dc] into next ch, rep from *, ending with 1dc into last ch, ch 3, turn.
Row 2: [1dc, ch 3, 1dc] into each 3ch sp, ending with 1dc into last ch, ch 3, turn.
Row 2 forms patt, rep for length of belt.

To make the skinny belt

Using yarns A and B together throughout and size 7 (4.5mm) hook, ch 8, turn.
Row 1: [1dc, ch 3, 1dc] into 5th ch from hook, sk 2ch, 1dc into last ch, ch 3, turn.
Row 2: [1dc, ch 3, 1dc] into 3ch sp, ending with 1dc into last ch, ch 3, turn.
Row 2 forms patt, rep for length of belt.

To finish

Using tapestry needle, weave in loose ends (see page 18). Using sewing needle, sew belt buckle to one end of length of fabric.

the skinny belt

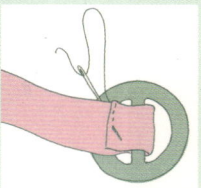

*T*his pretty skirt is worked in one piece and sewn together with a single side seam. The length can be adjusted by crocheting more or fewer rows. Line it or find a slip in a contrasting silk, and let the color shine through. Great for garden parties, walks in the park, and tennis (maybe).

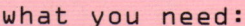

what you need:

tools:
size G/6 (4mm) crochet hook
tapestry needle
sewing needle & thread

materials:
7 x 1¾ oz./50g balls worsted yarn
*we used ggh Scarlett, shade 20 in Black (100% Egyptian cotton)
3 buttons
lining fabric: 3ft./1m x 5ft./1.5m

gauge:
1 patt repeat = 1½ in./4cm

measurements:
sizes = small (medium, large)
waist = 28 in./71cm (30 in./76cm, 32 in./81cm)
length = 22 in./56cm

To make the skirt

Using size G/6 (4mm) hook, ch 114 (120, 126).
Row 1: [3dc, ch 1, 3dc] into 6th ch from hook (1 shell formed), *sk 2ch, 1dc into next ch, sk 2ch, 1 shell into next ch, rep from * to end, ending with sk 2ch, 1dc into last ch, ch 3, turn.
Row 2: *[1 shell into center sp of next shell, 1dc into next dc] (patt rep made), rep from * to end, working last dc into top of turning ch, ch 3, 18 (19, 20) patt reps, turn.
Row 2 forms the patt, rep this row 6 more times.

Row 9 (Inc row): Work 2 patt reps but finish second rep with 3dc into dc, 1 shell into next shell, 3dc into dc, *work 5 (6, 6) patt reps but finishing last patt rep with 3dc into dc, work 1 shell into next shell.
Sizes small and large only: 1dc into dc, 1 shell into shell, then
All sizes: 3dc into dc, rep from * once more. Work 2 patt reps, working last dc into top of turning ch, ch 3, turn.

43

Row 10: Work 2 patt reps, work 1 shell into dc, 1dc into dc, 1 shell into shell, 1dc into dc, shell into dc, 1dc into dc, *work 5 (6, 6) patt reps, 1 shell into dc, 1dc into dc, work 1 shell into shell.
Sizes small and large only: 1dc into dc, 1 shell into shell, then
All sizes: 1dc into dc, 1 shell into dc, 1dc into dc. Rep from * once more. Work 2 patt reps, working last dc into top of turning ch, ch 3, turn. 24 (25, 26) patt reps.
Rep row 2 seven more times.
Row 17 (Inc row): Work 3 patt reps but finish second with 3dc into dc, work 1 shell into next shell, 3dc into dc, *work 7 (8, 8) patt reps but finishing last patt rep with 3dc into dc, work 1 shell into shell.
Sizes small and large only: 1dc into dc, 1 shell into shell, then
All sizes: 3dc into dc, rep from * once more, work 3 patt reps, working last dc into top of turning ch, ch 3, turn.
Row 18: Work 3 patt reps, work 1 shell into dc, 1dc into dc, 1 shell into shell, 1dc into dc, 1 shell into dc, 1dc into dc, *work 7 (8, 8) patt reps, 1 shell into dc, 1dc into dc, 1 shell into shell.
Sizes small and large only: 1dc into dc, 1 shell into shell, then
All sizes: 1dc into dc, 1 shell into dc, 1dc into dc, rep from * once more, work 3 patt reps, working last dc into top of turning ch. ch 3, turn 30 (31, 32) patt reps.
Rep row 2 until work measures 22 in./56cm. Fasten off.

To make the waistband

Attach yarn to one end of foundation ch at start of work. Work 111 (117, 125) sc evenly across edge, ch 6, turn.
Row 1: 1hdc into 4th ch from hook, 1hdc in each of next 2ch, 1hdc into each sc across row, ch 2, turn.
Row 2: 1hdc into each hdc to last 3 sts, ch 1, sk 1hdc, 1hdc into next hdc, 1hdc into turning ch, (buttonhole made) 1ch, turn.
Row 3: 1sc into first hdc, *sk 2hdc, 1 shell into next hdc, sk 2sc, 1sc into next hdc, rep from * to last 3 sts, sc into each st. Fasten off.

To make the button band

Attach yarn to edge of fabric at right angles to the last st of waistband. Work 26sc evenly along edge, ch 1, turn. Work another 3 rows of sc on these sts. Fasten off.

To finish

Weave in loose ends (see page 18). Sew together side seam from bottom of skirt to button band. Sew bottom edge of button band to opposite side of fabric. Attach button on waistband under buttonhole.
Sew 2 more buttons on button band, using lace spaces as buttonholes.

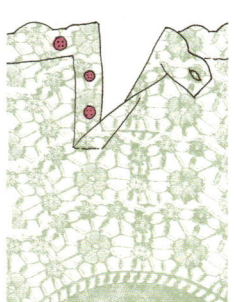

Placing the buttons

To make the lining

Lay skirt flat on large piece of paper and trace around edges. Remove skirt. Draw another line around side and bottom edges, ⅝ in./1.5cm from sides and 1¼ in./3cm from bottom. Put skirt back on pattern and mark position where skirt joins crochet waistband with dotted line. Cut around outer lines to make paper pattern.

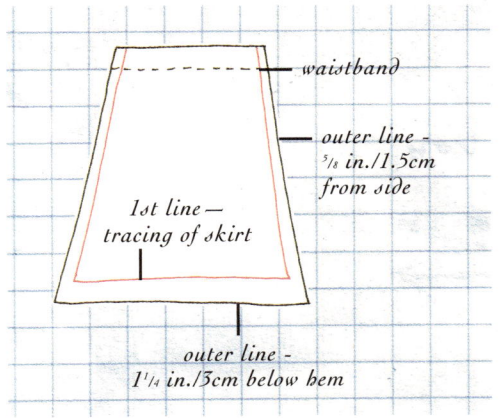

Paper pattern

Fold lining fabric in half and pin pattern on top, pinning through both layers of fabric. Cut around pattern and remove straight pins (2 pieces of fabric cut). Mark waistband position on both pieces of fabric with straight pins or row of running stitches.

Put 2 pieces of fabric right sides together and pin along side seams. Machine or hand sew both seams, using a ⅝ in./1.5cm seam allowance and leaving top of one seam open to match side opening of skirt. Trim each seam allowance to ⅜ in./1cm and finish raw edges with machine zigzag stitch or loose running stitches, making sure stitches are not visible on right side. Press seams open, turning down seam allowance at side opening.

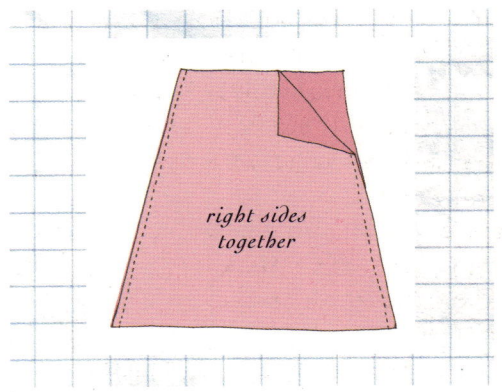

Sew side seams, leaving opening at top

Fold top edge to wrong side so that straight pins or runnings sts that mark waistband position are along fold. Cut folded-over waistband to ⅜ in./1cm and finish raw edges as before. Machine or hand stitch folded-over waistband in place. Fold under bottom edge by ⅜ in./1cm and press in place. Fold under again by ¾ in./2cm and pin in place. Machine or hand stitch around hem. Press lining.

Put lining inside skirt with wrong sides faceup, matching side openings of lining and skirt. Pin top edge of lining in place to match up with bottom of crochet waistband, gathering lining slightly if necessary. Hand stitch in place. Pin folded edge of lining side opening to side opening of skirt, making sure fabric isn't visible on right side. Hand stitch in place.

10 vest

Vests are wonderful, and this one has a particularly lovely neckline, scooped low and edged in the softest sky blue mohair. The main worsted yarn is soft and quick to work, and is decorated with a pretty flower motif at the hem. How can you live without it?

what you need:

tools:
sizes H/8 & G/6 (5mm & 4mm) crochet hooks
tapestry needle
sewing needle & thread

materials:
Yarn A: 4 (4, 5) x 1¾ oz./50g balls worsted yarn
*we used Lana Grossa Royal Tweed, shade 06 in Gray (100% fine merino)
Yarn B: 1 x 1 oz./25g ball fine mohair
*we used ggh Soft Kid, shade 57 in Cloudy Blue (70% super kid mohair, 25% nylon, 5% new wool)
5 round blue buttons

gauge:
11.5dc & 8 rows = 4 in./10cm

measurements:
sizes = small (medium, large)
bust = 31-34 in./81-86cm (35-36 in./90-91cm, 37-38 in./94-97cm)
length = 18 in./46cm

To make the back

Using yarn A and size H/8 (5mm) hook, ch 50 (55, 60), turn.
Row 1: 1dc into 4th ch from hook, 1dc into each of next ch to end, ch 3, turn, 47 (52, 57) sts.
Row 2: 1dc into each dc to end, ch 3, turn.
Rep row 2 until work measures 9½ in./24cm. Dec for armholes as follows:
Dec row 1: Sl st over 5 (6, 7) sts, 1dc into each of next sts to last 5 (6, 7) sts, leave these unworked, turn. 10 (12, 14) sts dec. 37 (40, 43) sts remain.
Dec row 2: Sl st over 3 sts, 1dc into each of next sts to last 3 sts, leave these unworked, turn. 6 sts dec. 31 (34, 37) sts remain.
Dec row 3: Dec 1 st at either end of row, 2 sts dec. 29 (32, 35) sts remain.
Work on these sts until work measures 18 in./46cm.
Shape the shoulders
Next row: Sl st over first st, 1sc into 2nd st, 1hdc into next st, 1dc into each of next 5 sts. Fasten off and attach yarn at other end of row to 2nd st, 1sc into 2nd st, 1hdc into next st, 1dc into each of next 5 sts. Fasten off.

To make the right front

Using yarn A and size H/8 (5mm) hook, ch 6, turn.
Row 1: 1dc into 4th ch from hook, 1dc into each of next chs, ch 3, turn. 3 sts.
Row 2: Dc across row, inc 2 sts at either end, ch 6 (7, 7), turn.
Row 3: 1dc into 4th ch from hook, 1dc into each of next chs, 1dc into each of next dc to end, inc 3 (4, 4) sts at end of row, ch 7, turn. 13 (15, 15) sts.

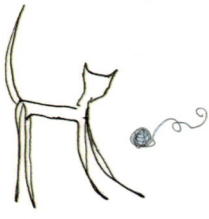

47

Row 4: 1dc into 4th ch from hook, 1dc into each of next 3 chs, 1dc into each of next dc to end, inc 4 sts at end of row, ch 3, turn. 21 (23, 23) sts.
Size large only:
Row 5: Dc across row, inc 1 st at either end, ch 3, turn. 25 sts.
Work another 7 in./18cm evenly.
Shape for neck as follows:
Row 1: Sl st along 2 sts, 1sc into 3rd st, dc to end, ch 3, turn. 19 (21, 23) sts.
Row 2: Dc to last 3 sts, 1sc in next st, turn. 17 (19, 21) sts.
Row 3: Dec 1 st at beg of row, dc to end, ch 3, turn. 16 (18, 20) sts.
Row 4: Dc to last 2 sts, dec 1 st, turn. 15 (17, 19) sts.
Start dec for armholes:
Row 5: Dec 1 st at beg of row, dc to last 4 sts, 1sc into next st, leave last 3 (3, 4) sts unworked, turn. 11 (13, 14 sts).
Row 6: Dec 2, (2, 3) sts at beg of row, dc to last 2 sts, dec 1 st. 8 (10, 10 sts).
Row 7: Dc across row.
Cont working in dc on these sts until armhole matches back, ending with wrong side row.
Shape the shoulder: With right side faceup, 1dc into each of first 5 sts, 1hdc into next st, 1sc into next st. Fasten off.

To make the left front

Using yarn A and size H/4 (5mm) hook, work as for right front for first 4 (4, 5) rows.
Work another 2 rows.
Make the flower as follows:
Row 1: 1dc into each of next 8 (10, 12) sts, ch 2, sk 1dc, 1tr into next st, ch 2, sk 1dc, dc to end of row, ch 3, turn.
Row 2: 1dc into each of next 7 (9, 11) sts, ch 5, sl st into tr of previous row, ch 5, sk 2ch and next dc, dc to end, ch 3, turn.
Row 3: 1dc into each of next 7 (9, 11) sts, 2dc into ch sp, ch 2, 1tr into sl st, ch 2, 2dc into ch sp, dc to end, ch 3, turn.
Row 4: Dec 1 st at beg of row, 1dc into each of next dc, 1dc into ch sp, 1dc into tr, 1dc into ch sp, dc to last 2 sts, dec 1 st, ch 3, turn. 21 (23, 25 sts).
Work evenly until work reaches the neck shaping as for right front.
Next row: Sl st over 2 sts, 1sc into 3rd st, 2dc into each of next dc to end, ch 3, turn. 19 (21, 23) sts.
Row 2: Dc to last 3 sts, 1sc into next st, leave last 2 sts unworked, turn. 17 (19, 21) sts.
Row 3: Dec 1 st at beg of row, dc to end of row, ch 3, turn. 16 (18, 20) sts.
Row 4: Dc to last 2 sts, dec 1 st, ch 3, turn. 15, (17, 19) sts.
Start dec for armholes:
Row 5: Dec 1 st at beg of row, dc to last 4 (4, 5) sts, 1sc into next st, leave last 3 (3, 4) sts unworked, turn. 11 (13, 14) sts.
Row 6: Dec 2 (2, 3) sts at beg of row, 1dc into each dc to last 2 sts, dec 1 st, ch 3, turn. 8 (10, 10) sts.
Cont on these sts until left front matches right front.
Shape the shoulder: With wrong side faceup, work 1dc into each of first 5 sts, 1hdc into next st, 1sc into next st. Fasten off.

To finish

Sew all seams together, starting with shoulder seams. Press lightly.
Attach yarn A to armhole edge and using size G/6 (4mm) hook, work 1 row of sc evenly around armhole. Rep at other side.
Attach yarn A to bottom of neck on right front and using size G/6 (4mm) hook, work 3 rows sc evenly around front edge including point, stopping at side seam.
Attach yarn A to bottom of neck on left front and using size G/6 (4mm) hook, work 2 rows sc evenly around front edge including point, stopping at side seam. Work another row of sc around this edge, making 5 buttonholes as follows evenly spaced along the front overlap: *4sc, ch 2, sk 2 sts, rep from * to make each buttonhole. Fasten off.
Attach yarn B to bottom of neck edge and using size G/6 (4mm) hook, work 1 row of sc around neck, making sure the finished number of sts is a multiple of 6, ch 1, turn.
Next row: Using size H/8 (5mm) hook, *[1sc into next st, sk 2sc, 6dc] (1 shell made) into next st, sk 2sc, rep from * to end. Fasten off.
Weave in loose ends (see page 18). Attach 5 buttons to right front to match the 5 buttonholes.

11 hood

what you need:

tools:
sizes H/8 & G/6 (5mm & 3.5mm) crochet hooks
tapestry needle
sewing needle & thread

materials:
Yarn A: 2 x 1¾ oz./50g balls DK yarn
*we used Jade Sapphire Mongolian Cashmere, shade 55 in Mahogany (100% cashmere)
Yarn B: 1 x 1¾ oz./50g ball DK yarn
*we used Debbie Bliss Cotton Cashmere, shade 56 in Green (85% cotton, 15% cashmere)
Yarn C: 1 x 1¾ oz./50g ball worsted yarn
*we used Debbie Bliss Alpaca Silk, shade 20 in Pink (80% alpaca, 20% silk)
1 button

gauge:
15 sts x 16 rows = 4 in./10cm

measurements:
to fit average head
tip to neck = 10 in./25.5cm

TO MAKE A PUFF (P1)

*Yo, insert hook into next st, yo, pull through a loose loop. Rep from * 4 more times. Yo. Pull loop through 10 loops on hook. 2 loops on hook. Yo and pull yarn through last 2 loops. Puff made (**P1**).

puff edging

What is special about this hood? Well . . . it has a cute pointy shape, fits like a dream, and is trimmed with a little puff edging that frames the face in the prettiest way. And we made it in the softest, warmest cashmere we could find. For cold days and snow pixies.

To make the hood

Using yarn A and size H/8 (5mm) hook, ch 76, turn.
Row 1: 1sc into 2nd ch from hook, 1sc in each ch to end, ch 1, turn. 75 sts.
Row 2: Sc to end, ch 1, turn. 75 sts.
Cont in this way for 22 more rows, turn.
Row 25: 1sc into next 2sc, [P1 in next sc, 1sc in next sc] twice, P1 in next sc, sc to last 7 sts, [P1 in next sc, 1sc in next sc] twice, P1 in next sc, sc to end, ch 1, turn.
Row 26: 1sc into each of next 8 sts, P1, work 1sc into each of next st to last 9 sts, P1, 1sc into each of last 8 sts, ch 1, turn.

Decrease rows:
Row 27: Sl st over first 5 sts, 1sc in each of next 5 sts, P1 in next st, sc to last 11 sts, P1 in next st, sc to last 5 sts, turn. 65 sts.
Row 28: Dec 2 sts at start of row, 1sc into each of next 4 sts, P1 in next st, sc to last 7 sts, P1 in next st, 1sc into each of foll st to last 2 sts, leave these unworked, turn. 61 sts.
Rep row 28 until there are 17 sts.
Next row: Dec 2 sts at start of row, 1sc into each of next 4 sts, [P1 in next st, 1sc in next st] twice, P1 in next stitch, 1sc into each of foll st to last 2 sts, leave these unworked, turn. 13 sts.
Next row: Dec 2 sts at both ends, turn. 9 sts.
Next row: Dec 1 st at both ends, turn. 7 sts.
Fasten off.

Fold hood in half, sew seam along foundation ch edge, which will make the back of the hood.
Using size H/8 (5mm) hook, join yarn A to bottom left along neck, with back of hood facing you. Work 42sc evenly across neck edge, ch 11 for strap, turn.
Work 1sc into 2nd ch from hook, work 9sc into each of foll ch and 1sc evenly across sc on neck edge to end, ch 1, turn.
Work 1sc in each sc to last 3 sts, ch 1, sk 1sc, 1sc in each of last 2sc (ch sp makes buttonhole), ch 1, turn.
Work 1sc in each st to end.
Fasten off yarn A.

To make the edging

Row 1: Join yarn B to one end of neck edge and work evenly across the whole edge of hood, making sure the final number of sts is a multiple of 4. Sl st to first sc to join row. Fasten off.
Row 2: Using size G/6 (3.5mm) hook, join yarn C to first st of first row of edging. *1sc into each of next 3sc, ch 4, remove hook from loop and reinsert into first of the 4 chs and then back into last ch, yo, pull loop through both chs on hook, rep from * across edge to last st, sl st into first sc of row to join. Fasten off.

To finish

Block into shape and weave in loose ends (see page 18).

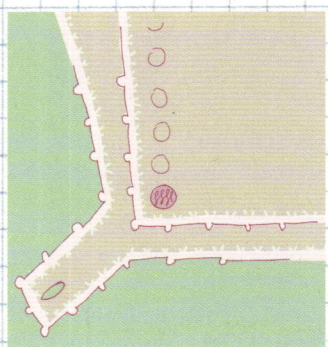

place button in line with puffs

12 throw

what you need:

tools:
size J/10 (6mm) crochet hook
tapestry needle

materials:
Yarn A: 16 (24) x 1¾ oz./50g balls DK yarn in 4 colors [4 (6) balls in each color]
*we used ggh Mystik (54% cotton, 46% rayon) in: shade 97 in Petrol Blue, shade 74 in Powder Blue, shade 69 in Pink, and shade 87 in Mint
**important: work all these yarns double (by holding 2 strands together throughout)
Yarn B: 3 (4) x 3½ oz./100g balls bulky yarn
*we used Rowan Chunky Print, shade 83 in Brown (100% pure new wool)
Yarn C: 1 x 1 oz./25g ball metallic yarn
*we used Twilleys Goldfingering in Silver (80% viscose, 20% metallized polyester)

gauge:
each motif = 6 in./15cm square

measurements:
small (25 squares) = 31 in. square/ 78cm²
large (49 squares) = 43 in. square/ 108cm²

This throw is made in squares and sewn together like a patchwork quilt. The pattern is derived from the traditional granny square, mixed together with bright striped squares in gorgeous iridescent yarns. To make a small throw, you need 5 granny squares (square 1s) and 20 striped squares (square 2s). For a large throw, make 5 square 1s and 44 square 2s.

To make square 1

Using yarn A in Pink and size J/10 (6mm) hook, ch 4, sl st to first ch to form a ring, ch 3.

Round 1: 2dc into ring, ch 2, [3dc in ring, ch 2] 3 times, join to top of beg 3ch with sl st. Fasten off Pink.

Round 2: Join yarn A in Petrol Blue to one corner sp, ch 3 to count as first dc, [2dc, ch 2, 3dc] into ch sp, ch 1, *[3dc, ch 2, 3dc] into next ch sp, ch 1, rep from * twice more, join with sl st to top of first 3ch. Fasten off Petrol Blue.

Round 3: Join yarn A in Powder Blue to one corner 2ch sp, ch 3 to count as first dc, [2dc, ch 2, 3dc] into ch sp, ch 1, 3 dc into next 1ch sp, ch 1, *[3dc, ch 2, 3dc] into next ch sp, ch 1, 3dc into next 1ch sp, ch 1, rep from * twice more, join with sl st to top of first 3ch. Do not turn. Fasten off Powder Blue.

Round 4: Join yarn B to one corner, 2ch sp, ch 3 to count as first dc, [2dc, ch 2, 3dc] into ch sp, ch 1, 3dc into next 1ch sp, ch 1, 3dc into next 1ch sp, ch 1, *[3dc, ch 2, 3dc] into next 2ch sp, ch 1, 3dc into next 1ch sp, 1ch, 3dc into next 1ch sp, ch 1, rep from * twice more, join with sl st to top of first 3ch. Fasten off yarn B and weave in loose ends.

Make 5 (5) alike, one for each corner and one for center of throw.

To make square 2

Work as follows, changing colors every row randomly between all of the yarns except yarn C.

Round 1: Using size J/10 (6mm) hook, ch 4, [1dc (ch 2, 3dc) 3 times, ch 2, 1dc] all in 4th ch from hook, join with sl st to 3rd ch of first 4ch.

Round 2: Ch 3, 1dc in next dc, *[2dc, ch 2, 2dc] in 2ch sp, dc in each of next 3dc, rep from * twice more, [2dc, ch 2, 2dc] in last 2ch sp, ending 1dc in next dc, join with sl st in top of first ch.

Round 3: Ch 3, 1dc into each of next 3dc, *[2dc, ch 2, 2dc] in 2ch sp, 1dc in each of next 7dc, rep from * twice more, [2dc, ch 2, 2dc] in last 2ch sp, ending 1dc in each of next 3dc, join with sl st to top of first 3ch.

Round 4: Ch 3, 1dc in each of next 5dc, *[2dc, ch 2, 2dc] in 2ch sp, 1dc in each of next 11dc, rep from * twice more, [2dc, ch 2, 2dc] in last 2ch sp, ending 1dc in each of next 5dc, join with sl st to top of first 3ch.

Fasten off and weave in loose ends.
Make 20 (44) squares in this way, randomly changing colors for every row of each square.

To finish

Follow the diagram below and sew all squares together with a slip stitch in a color yarn that blends in with the yarns used.

Fasten yarn C to the outside edge of the throw and using a size J/10 (6mm) hook, work 2 rows of sc evenly around the edge, so the final number of sts is a multiple of 4. Fasten off and attach yarn B. Using J/10 (6mm) hook, *ch 5, sk 3sc, 1sc into next sc, rep from * all around. Join round with sl st to bottom of first ch.
Weave in loose ends (see page 18).

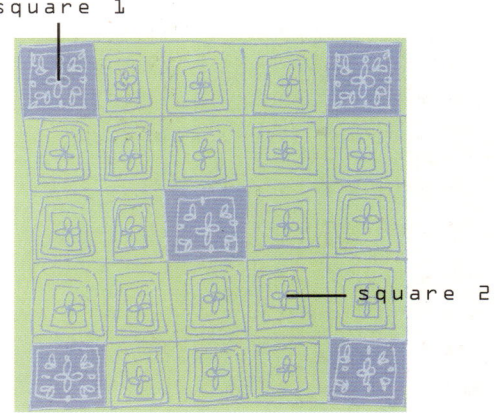

place square 1 motifs at center & in 4 corners

13 shrug

So simple....
SO simple....
....& OH SO lovely....

This shrug is made as a single piece, simply by changing the hook size to shape the cuffs. And you can add a glimpse of silver for decoration. The worsted yarn is luxurious and warm and great fun to use on a large hook. Ideal for beginners. Lovely on everyone.

To make the shrug

Using yarn A and size G/6 (4mm) hook, ch 51 (55, 59).
Row 1: 1hdc into 3rd ch from hook, 1hdc in each of next ch to end, ch 2, turn. 48, (52, 56) sts.
Row 2: Hdc to end, ch 2, turn.
Rep row 2 three more times. Fasten off.
Next row: Join in yarn B, ch 1, sc to end, turn. Fasten off.
Join in yarn A and work row 2 twice more, turn. Fasten off.

what you need:

tools:
sizes 10¼ & G/6 (6.5mm & 4mm) crochet hooks
tapestry needle

materials:
Yarn A: 5 (6, 6) x 1¾ oz./50g balls worsted yarn
*we used Rooster Almerino Aran, in Rooster (50% baby alpaca, 50% merino)
Yarn B: 1 x 1 oz./25g ball metallic yarn
*we used Twilleys Goldfingering, in Silver (80% viscose, 20% metallized polyester)

gauge:
16½ hdc x 12½ rows = 4 in./10cm
2½ V st x 6½ rows = 4 in./10cm

measurements:
sizes = small (medium, large)
bust = 31-34 in./81-86cm (35-36 in./90-91cm, 37-38 in./94-97cm)

Row 9: Join in yarn B, ch 1, sc to end, ch 1, turn.
Rep last row once more. Fasten off.
Join in yarn A and work row 2 three more times, ending last row with ch 3 to count as first dc on next row.
Change to size 10¼ (6.5mm) hook.
Row 14: Work 1 half V st into next hdc as follows: yo, insert hook into next st, yo, pull loop through, yo, pull yarn through 2 loops, yo, insert hook back into same st, yo, pull loop through, yo, pull yarn through 2 loops, yo, pull yarn through rem 3 loops on hook (1 half V st made), sk 3 sts, work 1 V st into next hdc as follows: 1dc into next st, ch 2, sl st into same st, ch 2, 1dc into same st (1 V st made), *sk 3 sts, work 1 V st into next hdc, rep from * to last 5 sts, sk 3 sts, 1 half V st into next hdc, 1dc into last st, ch 3, turn. 2 half V sts and 10 V sts made.

WRAP yourself **up**

Row 15: Work 1 V st into sp after half V st in last row, *1 V st into next sp between V sts, rep from *, ending with 1dc into turning ch, ch 3, turn. 11 V sts and 1dc at either end of row made.

Row 16: Work 1 half V st into sp before first V st on previous row, *work 1 V st into sp between next 2 V sts, rep from *, ending 1 half V st into sp after last V st on previous row, 1dc into turning ch, ch 3, turn.

Rows 15 and 16 form patt. Rep these rows until work measures approximately 26 (28, 30) in./65 (70, 75) cm, ending with a row 16.

Change back to size G/6 (4mm) hook.

Next row: 1hdc into top of half V st, *ch 3, 1hdc into top of V st, rep from * to last half V st, ch 3, 1hdc into top of half V st, 1hdc into turning ch 2, turn.

Next row: Hdc to end, ch 2, turn. 48 (52, 56) sts. Rep this row twice more. Fasten off.
Next row: Join in yarn B, sc to end, ch 1, turn. Rep last row once more. Fasten off.
Next row: Join in A, hdc to end, ch 2, turn. Rep last row once more. Fasten off.
Next row: Join in yarn B and work 1sc into each of next sts to end of row, ch 1, turn.
Next row: Join in yarn A, hdc to end, ch 2, turn. Rep last row 4 more times. Fasten off.

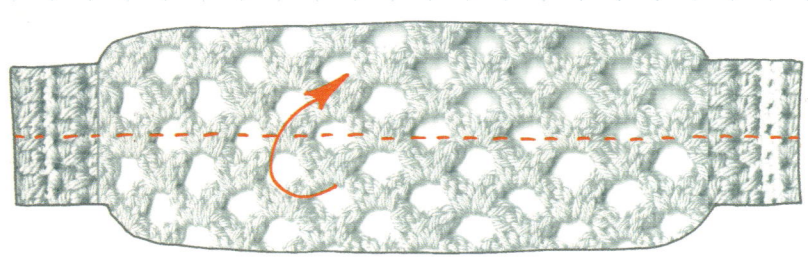

Fold shrug along its length

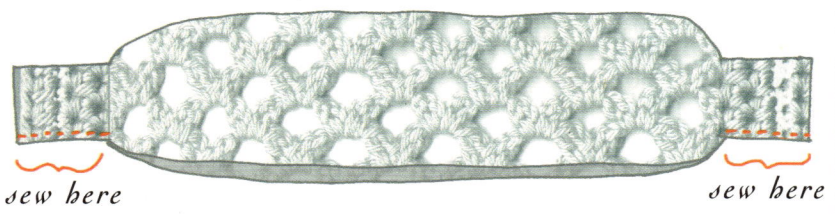

Sew together the 13 hdc rows at either end to make sleeves, leaving the V-st fabric unsewn to make the body.

To finish

Fold piece in half widthwise and sew together only the 13 hdc rows at either end to make sleeves, leaving the V-st fabric unsewn to make the body.

To make the edging

Using yarn A and size G/6 (4mm) hook, attach yarn to the edge of V-st fabric and work one row of hdc evenly around this edge, in a large circle, until you are back to where you joined in the yarn. Join around with a sl st to top of first st, ch 2. You will not have to turn from now on, you will be working in the round, around the edge of the V-st fabric.
Join rounds with a sl st to first st in each round. Work 2 more rounds of hdc in yarn A. Fasten off yarn A and join in yarn B.
Work 2 rounds of sc in yarn B. Fasten off yarn B and join in yarn A.
Work 2 rounds of hdc in yarn A. Fasten off yarn A and join in yarn B.
Work 1 round of sc in yarn B. Fasten off yarn B and join in yarn A. Work 1 round of hdc in yarn A. Fasten off.

To finish

Weave in loose ends (see page 18).
Wear it and LOVE it!

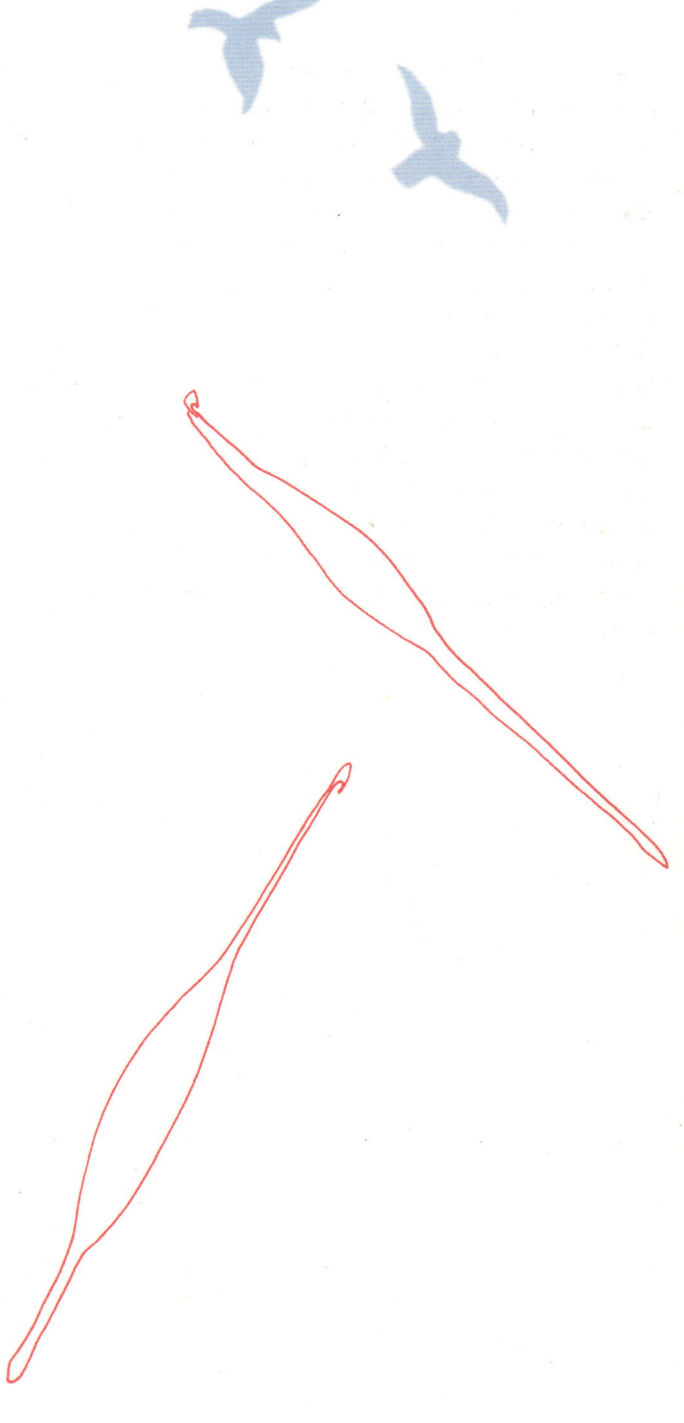

14 bluebird lavender cushion

Who wouldn't fall in love with a bluebird smelling of lavender? For this project, the motifs are made separately and sewn onto a bird-shaped cushion. You need 26 large blue flowers, 2 small blue flowers, 28 pink circles, and 22 blue circles. Oh—and 1 cushion shaped like a bird.

To make the large flowers

Using yarn B and size C/2 (2.5mm) hook, wrap yarn around little finger (or knitting needle) 18 times.
Round 1: Work 16sc evenly into ring made until all wrapped yarn is covered, join with a sl st to first sc.
Round 2: Ch 6, *sk 1sc, 1dc into next sc, ch 3, rep from * all around, ending with sl st into 3rd st of first ch to close round. 8 ch spaces.
Round 3: *[1dc, 1tr, 1dtr, 1tr, 1dc] into next ch sp, 1sc into next dc, rep from * to end of round, join with a sl st to first st of round. 8 petals. Fasten off. Make 26.

To make the circles

Using C/2 (2.5mm) hook, wrap yarn around little finger (or knitting needle) 18 times.
Round 1: Work sc evenly into ring made until all wrapped yarn is covered, join with a sl st to first sc. Fasten off.
Make 28 pink and 22 blue.

what you need:
tools:
size C/2 (2.5mm) crochet hook
tapestry needle
size 15 (10mm) knitting needle
sewing needle & thread

materials:
Yarn A: 1 x 1¾ oz./50g ball DK yarn
*we used ggh Mystik, shade 68 in Fuchsia (54% cotton, 46% rayon)
Yarn B: 1 x 1¾ oz./50g ball DK yarn
*we used Debbie Bliss Pure Silk, shade 07 in Blue (100% silk)
20 in./50cm white lining fabric
lavender + polyester fiber for cushion
2 glass or pearl buttons

gauge:
Not critical for this project

measurements:
large flower = 2½ in./6cm diameter
small flower = 1½ in./4cm diameter
circle = ¾ in./2cm diameter

To make the small flowers

Using yarn B and size C/2 (2.5mm) hook, wrap yarn around little finger (or knitting needle) 18 times.
Round 1: Work 16sc evenly into ring made until all wrapped yarn is covered. Join with a sl st to first sc. Do not turn.
Round 2: *Work [1dc, 1tr, 1dc] all into next sc, 1sc into next sc, rep from * to end of round, join with a sl st to first st of round. 8 points. Fasten off. Make 2.

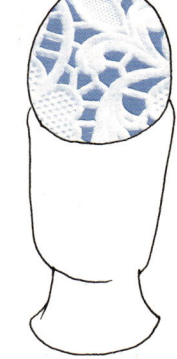

To finish

Weave in loose ends of motifs (see page 18).

Scale up template (p. 63) to approximately 12 in./30cm square using graph paper or a photocopier. Cut out 2 bird shapes from the fabric using the template. Put the bird shapes right sides together and sew around the edges, leaving a gap to add filling (note: template includes seam allowance of $\frac{5}{8}$ in./1.5cm). Turn to right side and fill with a mixture of lavender and polyester fiber. Sew up the gap.

Stitch the motifs to the fabric, randomly or in a repeat pattern, but touching, as in picture. You may have some motifs left over, depending on your arrangement.

Sew on 2 buttons for eyes.

template for the bluebird
scale up to 12 in. square/30cm²
(template includes seam allowance of ⅝ in./1.5cm)

Many thanks to: Catie Ziller for her original idea & clear guidance; Kathy Steer & Claire Montgomerie for their hard work & advice; Ben & Ruth for the photos; Mary & John, Dusty & Anne for all sorts of things; & . . .

First published in the United States in 2007 by
Watson-Guptill Publications
a division of VNU Business Media, Inc.
770 Broadway, New York, NY 10003
www.watsonguptill.com

Library of Congress Control Number: 2006936849

ISBN-10: 0-8230-9981-4
ISBN-13: 978-0-8230-9981-8

All rights reserved. No part of this publication may be reproduced or used in any form or by any means—graphic, electronic, or mechanical, including photocopying, recording, taping, or information storage and retrieval systems—without written permission of the publisher.

First published in France by Marabout (Hachette Livre) in 2006
© 2006 Marabout (Hachette Livre)

Printed in China

First printing, 2007

1 2 3 4 5 6 7 8 / 14 13 12 11 10 09 08 07